Testimonials & R

"It's very simple, Catherine: **YOU NAILED IT!**

ATTITUDE + ATTENTION = TEAMWORK! Seven steps to Success is simply outstanding. I've been in competition obedience for a quarter century and I've never encountered a book like this. Catherine doesn't tell you how to teach scent articles. She doesn't explain how to make Phydeaux proficient at weave poles. There's not one word about what you can and can't do with your hands and arms in rally.

Catherine's book is 195 pages of words and photos about how to CONNECT with your dog. How to build competitive excellence through teamwork. AND SHE NAILS IT!!

I have the book. I've read it and highlighted it. And I've gotten zinged several times about my own bad habits. (And am motivated to shape up.)

I highly recommend ATTITUDE + ATTENTION = TEAMWORK.

— **WILLARD BAILEY,** author of *Remembering to Breathe: Inside Dog Obedience Competition*
and *OTCH Dreams: The Agony and Ecstasy of Life with Competition Obedience Dogs.*

"Catherine Zinsky's book on developing attitude, attention and teamwork is a valuable addition to every dog lover's library. It's an easy read, and represents a well written, organized, thought provoking and informative approach to the fundamental requirements for building a competitive team (human/canine) in any dog sport. Dog sport newcomers and veterans alike will find the seven-step approach she outlines is easy to follow and represents key considerations in teambuilding. I am delighted to recommend this publication to any and every participant regardless of the chosen sport."

— **WARD FALKNER Ph.D.** (Zoology) Two-time winner of the AKC/Eukanuba National Obedience Championship & twice ranked #1 All Breeds Obedience Winner – Canadian Kennel Club

"This book is not about how to train your dog, but more about how to train yourself. I wish I'd had this book when I started training! I'd been doing so many things I shouldn't, and not doing so many things I should. It was no wonder there was a hole in my teamwork. This book isn't about training your dog, it's about training <u>you</u> so you don't make mistakes that cause a breakdown in your training. Building Attitude and Attention naturally leads to better Teamwork – the three most important things you and your dog need to take into the ring. The book is beautifully laid out leading you on a step by step journey to more Attitude and Attention with your dog. Building the Attitude and Attention naturally improves your relationship with your dog, and that leads to improved teamwork. This is the perfect book for new trainers, someone training a new dog (or puppy) and even experienced trainers. It is also a valuable tool for experienced trainers. I can't recommend it highly enough."

— **RUTHANN McCAULLEY,** Author of *"Rally All Around,"* Sierra Vista, AZ
IntlCH Dunham Lake Sticky Beak RN CGC NTD

"Another post for my "dog" friends. This is my review of the new book written by Catherine Zinsky titled *Attitude + Attention = TEAMWORK, Seven Steps to Success*. In my opinion Catherine scores a 200 with her new book! Get it! Read it! You won't learn about how to teach specific skills/exercises...rather she focuses on the handler's role in creating a winning team. She puts the responsibility for attitude and attention directly on the handler's shoulder—no excuses allowed! And she tells you HOW to be the best handler you can be for your particular dog. Very motivational. It is an easy read...195 pages of big print for those of us with less than perfect vision, and spiral bound. Worth every penny! Am so glad I bought this book. You can order it on her web site."

— **KATHYRYN MIELE**

"Catherine Zinsky's new book is a must for those that own and train dogs. *Attitude + Attention = Teamwork! Seven Steps to Success* is a well-written book of tips, guidelines and thoughtful discussion of Catherine's philosophy and techniques for creating teamwork with your dog. Each chapter supports Catherine's objective that the handlers' attitude and attention are essential in training in order to establish teamwork so critical for achieving success with your dog as a performance partner or even just a good friend to enjoy life with.

"Chapter 1 on leadership and working with puppies was one of my favorite chapters. In this chapter Catherine stresses the importance of teaching your dog to respond on the first command. To me, this is where so many of dogs problems arise when people do not understand how to deal with a distracted puppy, or dog who will not come when called or display the 'don't wanna, don't have to' behavior.

"The other 6 chapters are filled with excellent information to help you improve your relationship and teamwork with you dog. Chapter titles include: Canine Trinity: The Perfect Picture – be clear, be consistent: Praise and Errant Praise: Play and Interaction – never allow your dog to ignore you: Train, Train, Train – be honest and be fair: and Becoming the Ring Master – most importantly believe in yourself and enjoy the process.

"As an instructional designer and author/publisher I am very critical of educational books and online courses. I found Catherine's book to be very well written, well organized, with introductions to what the reader will learn in the chapter, excellent examples, how to correct unwanted behaviors, and chapter summaries and reviews. Well done Catherine!!!"

— **CYNDE LESHIN** (Cynde has worked in the health care field for over 10 years, is an author, instructional designer and most recently has become a faculty member in the College of Education at Western Governors University.)

"After reading many books and training dogs for over 20 years, I find *Attitude+Attention=Teamwork* to be one of the best new books to come along. It is easy to follow and combines practical advise with clear writing. The book is written in chapters and sections, with important points set apart. It is a great reference with a wealth of ideas for any level of training and all breeds. I am excited to start out using training ideas for my puppy as well as implement problem solving methods for my advanced open and utility dogs."
— **ANN MARIE GOLDHAMMER**

"CONGRATULATIONS!! You have a winner!!!! I so enjoyed reading your book. Something for everyone. For those just starting out to the more experienced handle. I liked all the photos. I know it was a big undertaking but you should be very proud of the out come." — **BETTY CUNNINGHAM**

"I was getting so frustrated with training that my dog wasn't enjoying it anymore, but I hadn't realized what the problem was. It was me! Catherine's book tells how important the trainer's attitude makes in the whole process of you & your dog being a happy and successful team." — **PAULINE ANDRUS**, AKC Obedience Judge

"Got home from the match and your book had arrived. I am already on page 38. I can't wait to tell my students about your book! Maybe they will pay attention to you when you say "say it once". ☺ I am glad it is raining so I will have an excuse to sit and read tomorrow after the tracking test." — **LORA COX**, AKC Obedience Judge

"I got your book today…I have to say you did a wonderful job, I love it, you have put in writing what I have always believed and tried to do. I showed it to a friend of mine and she wants to order one."
— **LOUISE BASTIEN**

"Just received my copy... What a beautiful book! It has much more than I expected. Instead of another "how to" teach exercises book, it goes in depth about the importance of bonding with your dog and achieving real teamwork. Thank you, Catherine, for your valuable contribution to us dog trainers. Good job, well done! Bravo!" — **CHRIS WALLACE**

"Your book is outstanding! Wish we had a copy years ago as it would have been a valuable tool with beloved pets in the past. Wishing you much success with your excellent book." — **VALERIE ROBERTSON**

ATTITUDE + ATTENTION = TEAMWORK!
Seven Steps to Success

By Catherine L. Zinsky

© 2015 • www.gettoready.net

Copyright © 2015 by Catherine L. Zinsky

All rights reserved. No part of this book may be reproduced or transmitted in any form or by any means, electronic or mechanical, including photocopying, recording or by any information storage and retrieval system, without the prior written permission of Catherine L. Zinsky.

All photos are credited to Catherine L. Zinsky unless otherwise noted.

Cover Photo: OTCH Sporting Field's Summer Solstice, UDX 8, OGM

Disclaimer

Mention of products in this book does not imply their endorsement by the author. Products appearing in a photograph in this book are not endorsed, explicitly or implicitly, by the author, photographers, or persons appearing in the same photograph.

The methods and techniques described in this book are subject to change without notice. The author assumes no responsibility for errors that may appear in this book or any damages that may arise from the use of the methods and techniques described in this book.

ISBN: 978-0-692-61601-7

Printed in the United States of America

Library of Congress Cataloging Pending

Published by Catherine L. Zinsky

www.gettoready.net

Printed by Upton Graphics

Bow-wows

This book is dedicated to all of the dogs I have known and loved, past and present. They taught me so much...

Special thanks go to Ruth Anderson-Barnett and Jennifer Kipper for their proofing and formatting assistance, and to Kathy Upton for her lay-out expertise, graphic design, and extraordinary patience working with me. This book couldn't have happened without her.
Much appreciated!

Most of all I want to thank my husband, John Saetti, for his untiring support, encouragement, objectivity and conviction.
Thank you, my love.

This book is dedicated to:

Ch. O.T.Ch. Trumagik Step Aside, UDX 20, OGM

2002-2015

Forever in my heart...

Table of Contents

About the Author iv

How It Works v

Chapter 1: LEADERSHIP 1
1.1 Every Team Needs a Leader 1
1.2 Leadership Begins at Home 3
1.3 Establishing the Pecking Order 5
1.4 Teach First 8
    1.4.1 Food Management 8
    1.4.2 Belly Up! 9
    1.4.3 Redirection 10
1.5 Manners Count! 12
    1.5.1 Teach First 12
1.6 Test Yourself 14
1.7 Handy Behaviors to Teach to Establish Home Rule 15
    1.7.1 Teaching 'Leave it' 17
1.8 The Bond that Binds 18
1.9 Redirect Unwanted Behaviors—Now! 21
1.10 Games that Bond 22
1.11 Chapter Review 28

Chapter 2: CANINE TRINITY™ 31
2.1 What Big EYES You Have! 33
    2.1.1 Things to 'Look' Out for 36
2.2 What Big EARS You Have! 38
2.3 What a Big NOSE You Have! 42
    2.3.1 Ideas to Redirect Negative Emotions 43
2.4 Chapter Review 55

Chapter 3: THE PERFECT PICTURE 57
3.1 Visualizing Your Objective 57
3.2 Why Have a *Perfect Picture*? 58
3.3 What Does it Mean to 'Go Through the Motions'? 61

3.4	Avoiding Ruts	63
3.5	Clarity in Training	66
3.6	Consistency in Training	69
3.7	Chapter Review	72

Chapter 4: PRAISE—AND ERRANT PRAISE 73

4.1	Praise is Essential!	73
4.2	What is Praise?	74
4.3	Learn to Listen to Yourself	75
4.4	Lure vs. Reward	77
4.5	Reward With Interaction	80
4.6	Bribe vs. Reward	82
4.7	Four Stage Release	84
4.8	Errant Praise	90
	4.8.1 Blanket Praise	91
	4.8.2 Praising Inaccuracies	94
	4.8.3 Misplaced Praise	95
4.9	Chapter Review	98

Chapter 5: PLAY & INTERACTION 99

5.1	Inspiring the "Want to"	99
5.2	Pressure Valve Release System	100
5.3	What is Interactive?	101
5.4	What is Self-Amusement?	104
5.5	Self-Amusement NOT!	105
5.6	Sustaining Attention	109
5.7	The Importance of Play	111
5.8	The 3 to 5 Approach	112
5.9	Attention Games	114
5.10	Toy at the Ready	123
5.11	How to Play!	125
5.12	Getting a Quick Release	128
5.13	Chapter Review	131

Chapter 6: TRAIN, TRAIN, TRAIN 133

6.1	Routine Required	133
6.2	Practice with Attention	134

6.3	My Dog is Bored-NOT!	135
6.4	*Training Alive!*™	139
6.5	To Drill or Not to Drill?	144
6.6	Downtimes	145
6.7	Doodling with S.O.S.	146
6.8	Quality vs. Quantity	152
6.9	Run-throughs	154
6.10	Chapter Review	156

Chapter 7: Becoming the Ring Master! 157

7.1	Partnership Required	159
7.2	Preparation: A Key Ingredient	160
7.3	Desensitize to Trial Environment	161
7.4	Finding Your "Show Gauge"	166
7.5	To Enter or Not to Enter? That is the Question	168
7.6	The "Goldilocks" Syndrome	169
7.7	Before the Trial Day	171
7.8	It's Showtime!	172
	7.8.1 Arrive Early	173
	7.8.2 Set Up for Success!	173
	7.8.3 The "Right Stuff"	174
	7.8.4 Get Organized	176
	7.8.5 Warm-Ups	179
	7.8.6 The Right Mind Set	181
7.9	Approach to the Ring	182
7.10	Crossing the Threshold	183
7.11	The Unforeseen Delay	185
7.12	Praise in the Ring?	186
7.13	Enjoy the Process!	188
7.14	Jackpot!	190
7.15	Chapter Review	192

A FINAL WAG 194

Chapter Recap & Reminders 195

About the Author...

Catherine has trained Dobermans, Cattle Dogs, and now Border Collies for nearly 40 years and has been actively exhibiting in AKC, UKC, and ASCA trials during that period. She has achieved multiple AKC championships in both conformation and obedience and has dabbled in agility, although obedience training and competition are her main focus and interest. Catherine has shown and placed at AKC National Invitational Competitions, State Top Dog Competitions, has been awarded more than 200 High in Trials (including at National Breed competitions), over 100 High Combined wins, and more than 20 perfect '200' scores. She is also an ASCA obedience trial judge and periodically presents obedience seminars for clubs throughout the nation.

Catherine had the honor to have been interviewed by both *Dog Sport Magazine* and the National Border Collie Magazine, *Borderlines*, for her achievements (2008 & 2009). She was then requested to write obedience articles regularly for *Dog Sport Magazine*. This arrangement continued for four years. Additionally, she writes a monthly column for *Front and Finish, The Dog Trainer's News* entitled "Playing by the Rules," which she has written for over twelve years. Catherine has also been published in *Borderlines* and in the *Cattle Dog* newsletter, All Breed Obedience Club's newsletter, *Dog Daze*, and in Hidden Valley Obedience Club's newsletter, *Come For News*.

The author's philosophy in dog training sounds simple: be fair and honest. Being fair and honest is, however, not nearly as simple as it sounds. When working with dogs and teaching any given skill or part of any skill, her ultimate goal is to have the dog truly understand what is being asked. Catherine believes that this understanding allows for greater confidence and flexibility in the dog. A dog that understands and who has confidence is a dog that will enjoy showing and will enjoy performing his entire life.

Ultimately her desire—through teaching, writing for *Front and Finish Dog Magazine,* providing a "Competitive Obedience Toolbox" on her website, www.gettoready.net, and the publication of this book—is to help others develop a deeper understanding of the trainer/canine bond and in so doing, have a more rewarding relationship and greater success.

How It Works...

My goal in this manual is to show you how to achieve teamwork with your dog. I have formulated a seven-step program that will provide you with a positive, forward approach towards establishing true teamwork.

Each chapter represents one of these steps. **NO STEP CAN STAND ALONE**, but must be employed in combination with all of the other steps in order to be successful and ultimately achieve true teamwork.

To select only one chapter and exclude the others would be like making a cake without using all of the ingredients. Each step, each chapter, is dependent upon the previous and can only become a 'cake' if all seven are put into the batter, so to speak. Teamwork gradually advances with the coming together of all of these seven ingredients.

Please note: this is not a dog training book. Specific performance techniques are NOT a part of this program. (To train for Agility or Obedience, etc., I highly recommend you contact your nearest dog club.)

It's important to understand that having a dog that is trained and having teamwork are not the same. Many dogs at performance trials have at least some degree of training, yet are unable to function or follow direction when performing. ***Teamwork is absent.***

Teamwork is a union between players. Teamwork is a cohesion and accord, affording the players the chance to work as one unit. There is a tacit understanding and feeling that comes through working together that frees each member to ebb and flow as required, as needed. This allows for harmony and smoothness. ***This is teamwork.***

We all want our dogs to be looking at us attentively with a positive, anxious attitude asking, "What's next? Let's do it!" We ask attention and attitude from them, but too often fail to give it in return. As a consequence, teamwork becomes impossible.

Every topic, every chapter, is directed at the trainer/handler. It is my belief—and premise in this book—that fundamentally dogs want to be with us and are in varying degrees highly trainable.

My objective is to demonstrate the importance of the handler's attitude and attention as well as to show how you, the handler/trainer, can increase your **attention** to your dog and amplify your own **attitude** in training in order to establish true **teamwork**.

No matter what venue you hope to compete in, teamwork is a must. But more important is achieving that unity, that oneness with your canine buddy

v

that can only be gotten through the bond that grows from mutual understanding, respect, and time well-spent together.

Hopefully by following the seven-step process presented in this manual, you will develop a deeper understanding of your dog and his needs—as well as a greater understanding of yourself. This can only serve to make you a better trainer overall.

Got treats?

Pardon My Pronouns....

In order to simplify and make reading this manual go more smoothly, I have opted to refer to all dogs as 'he' and all trainers as 'she.' Please do not take offense. This is merely my way of avoiding saying 'he/she' throughout, which would be quite cumbersome. Only when the gender is specifically known do I divert from this approach. Thank you for your understanding.

Photo by Kit Rodwell

*Chinese Proverb: If you tell me, I'll soon forget.
If you show me, I'll remember forever.*

Chapter One: LEADERSHIP

What to expect in this chapter:

- What leadership means
- Leadership begins at home
- Establishing a pecking order
- Do's and Don'ts
- Food management for leadership
- Teaching manners
- Building a bond
- Teaching through redirection
- Games to build your relationship
- Chapter Review

Leadership is perhaps **the** most important ingredient to teamwork—and is most certainly your first and most constant step towards establishing real harmony. Leadership is the act of guiding and directing, of making decisions and pointing the way, of inspiring while also being in command.

Leadership as it pertains to a human/canine relationship is two-fold:

1. Pack leadership.
2. Team leadership.

Pack leadership is primary: team leadership is dependent upon pack leadership and is a union that evolves as you and your dog learn and grow together.

Let's first examine what a team is, then pack leadership and ways to establish it. After that begins the journey of building team leadership…

1.1 Every team needs a leader…

> *There isn't a team on the planet that doesn't have a leader.*
>
> ***No leader, no team: it's that simple.***

Being the leader is YOUR job when training your dog for whichever performance event you have chosen.

Team leader examples:
- ✦ An orchestra has a conductor
- ✦ A football team has a coach
- ✦ An ice-skating team has a lead partner
- ✦ A dance team has a lead partner
- ✦ A battalion has its General
- ✦ A wolf pack has a pack leader

Wherever there is a team, someone is in charge!

The football coach gives the players leadership, cohesion, direction, and purpose. Without the coach—the team leader—there can be no team. The coach gives the team means and method, trains them, presents a game plan, bolsters their confidence and gives them moral support. Without the coach there would be no direction , there could be no unity, no management, no leader to **MAKE THEM A TEAM.**

A conductor gives the orchestra unity and harmony: no conductor, no harmony.

The leader of an ice-skating pair brings smoothness and the illusion of effortlessness. The pair will be in step and move as one: with no leader they would collide, crash and burn…

It is exactly the same with you and your dog: your dog needs a leader to direct, to bring smoothness, stability, and understanding. Without a leader your dog will lack direction, purpose, even understanding. There will be no unity, only confusion. Certainly NOT teamwork.

- ✓ Should you **not** take the lead when working with your dog, rest assured that your dog will gladly step into that role! Unfortunately his agenda will NOT be yours.

Remember: NO LEADER, NO TEAM: it's that simple.

1.2 Leadership Begins At Home...

Leadership begins at home the moment your puppy enters your life: leadership is not something that evolves down the road when you finally decide to compete.

What does leadership mean exactly, as it pertains to your dog and your household?

- ✦ Does it mean the dog has to sleep outside? No, of course not.
- ✦ Does it mean that the dog can't be allowed on the sofa? Again, no.
- ✦ Does it mean that the dog has to be whipped into submission? **Heaven forbid!**

Being a bully does not make a leader. Leadership is an attitude, not physical suppression.

Being a leader means that you are in charge and that you direct the performance and activities in any given situation—and it all starts on the home front.

It's essential to recognize that dogs are pack animals. They are descendants of the wolf. Wolves run in packs. In order for the pack to work together and survive, it requires a leader—and every wolf pack has a leader, hands down.

A dog's genetic makeup is programmed for pack mentality. When a puppy enters your household, you are establishing a pack—even if that pack is only you and the puppy. The number of members is unimportant. What is important is that in the puppy's mind you are a member of his family, and so are a member of the pack. How the relationship develops between you and your new dog is going to decide who will ultimately be pack leader.

This pup is serious...he seriously wants to be pack leader. This is a natural behavior, but one you, as the master, must supersede.
YOU MUST ESTABLISH YOUR POSITION AS LEADER.

Who will be the leader should not be optional! It MUST be you!

It's tremendously important to recognize that dogs are not humans. Dogs have different genes, different DNA, and so have different 'programming', if you will. If you don't accept these differences and allow the dog to follow his natural, genetic instincts, then you are doing your dog a great disservice.

A dog that does not have a clear picture of his role within the family (his pack) is a confused dog. He may be aware of certain household limitations, though even these won't be crystal clear, which only adds to the confusion base. This could be the dog that...

- Still urinates occasionally in the house.
- Is destructive.
- Only 'comes' on the third, and now 'harsh' command.
- Doesn't get down off the couch until threatened.
- Refuses to move or even acknowledge you as you step over him.
- Controls all 'play' situations: the what and when and how often.

Gray areas for a dog can cause much confusion. Be kind: establish the home ground rules for your dog and be very clear as to want you expect. And then toss in consistency to guarantee harmony.

Once you gain the respect of your dog on the home front—and it all begins by your establishing the pecking order and letting your dog know that you are captain of the ship—becoming the team leader in your chosen performance venue will not only be more straightforward, it will be more enjoyable for you both.

1.3   ESTABLISHING THE PECKING ORDER

Initially your puppy is going to be extremely compliant and eager to follow you and do what he does best: be cute.

But there will come a time when that puppy is going to start testing the waters to see what it can and cannot get away with.

Do not attribute a puppy's naughtiness to 'just being a puppy.' Instead, ask yourself, "Is this a behavior I want my adult dog to have?"

REMEMBER: a puppy wants the best of all possible worlds, and naturally from the puppy's prospective what is best for the puppy is to be in charge. When he's in charge, he gets what HE wants. He will become the leader and do all of the decision making.

*This is not a healthy situation,
nor is it favorable for teamwork.*

Your future performance dog needs to understand and accept you as the team leader, and this respect can only begin at home.

It's really not as difficult as some think. There are many different approaches, but here are some dos and don'ts that can get you started on the right path.

Things You Can Do....

- ✓ Have your dog sit and wait for his dinner. Always!

- ✓ Be able to take the food dish away at anytime while he is eating.

- ✓ Crate train your dog.

- ✓ Train your dog to also sit and wait until you give the okay for:

  — Going out the front door

  — Getting out of his crate

  — Getting out of the car

  — Receiving any special treat

- ✓ Be able to remove any object or food item (cookie, bone, chew toy, stick) from your dog's mouth.

- ✓ Ensure, once a behavior is taught, that your dog responds to your <u>first</u> command, whatever it might be.

- ✓ Teach your dog to walk nicely beside you.

- ✓ Insist that the dog move out of your way should you need to pass (that is, you do not step over him or try to sidestep around him).

It's mandatory that you immediately put the kibosh on any and all behaviors that you aren't happy with. After all, it's your household, your furniture, and your harmony that is being challenged here. Do not allow it to be jeopardized.

Unacceptable Behaviors:

- ✓ Does not come when called *the first time*.
- ✓ Jumps onto the kitchen counter.
- ✓ Begs at the table.
- ✓ Curls a lip at you under ANY circumstances.
- ✓ Makes low 'warning' growls.
- ✓ Nips at your heels.
- ✓ Refuses to be handled or groomed.
- ✓ When walking/exercising, 'marks' the entire route.
- ✓ Dictates play sessions: he chooses when and what toy.
- ✓ Is destructive.
- ✓ Barks excessively.

Stop all unwanted behaviors during puppy-hood.

1.4 TEACH FIRST!

Your responsibility as pack leader is to show and teach your dog how to become an effective family member. It isn't fair to ask a dog to behave in an agreeable fashion if he has never been taught what is acceptable and what is not. Dogs are not mind readers. They cannot second guess you.

1.4.1 Food Management.

Managing your dog's food distribution is an excellent first step. It's crucial that your dog understand that the food is yours and that you are sharing it with him. You are in charge of the meal: it is yours to give and it is yours to take away.

Glimmer waits patiently to be released to eat.

Demonstrating this reality to your dog should begin the day your dog enters your household.

Until you are able to teach a sit/stay, simply hold the puppy back by his collar or harness. Place the food down. Release your hold, give a verbal 'Okay,' and allow the puppy to eat a bit, then reach down and remove the dish.

Your puppy should willingly accept your interference. If he does not, give the collar a quick check (shake) and tell him to knock it off. Repeat the entire procedure. Do this every day for 2-6 weeks, depending upon the dog and the dog's response.

You might also periodically put your hand into (or over) the dog's food just to remind him that it is yours and that you are sharing it with him.

If you have a truly resentful pup, you might try hand feeding each piece of food until the pup accepts your leadership.

Apply this 'give and take' approach toward toys, bones, or any other object your pup enjoys holding in his mouth. It is essential that your dog understand that you are in charge, you are his leader.

Furthermore, the puppy will quickly learn that all good things—food, toys, praise—come from you. You will soon become the most important person in his world.

1.4.2 Belly Up!

Another safe, inoffensive but simple way to establish your authority as leader is to pick up your puppy and hold him on his back (belly upwards) in your arms. Should the puppy squirm or fuss or worse, throw a tantrum, do <u>not</u> release the puppy until he settles in and accepts this position. Your puppy <u>must</u> accept and demonstrate submissiveness to your authority. Once he calms down, reward him with soothing words and praise.

For a large puppy or an older dog, have him lie down, then gently roll him over onto his back and have him remain in this position until released.

Again, do <u>not</u> release him if he resists: only release him once he has stopped squirming and accepts your authority.

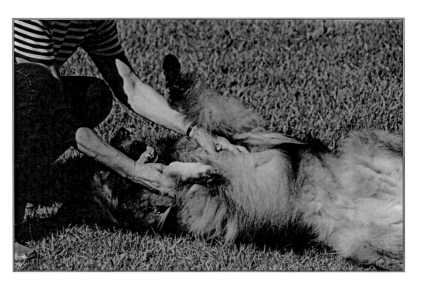

1.4.3 Redirection.

<u>Redirection</u> is a wonderful way to offset bad behaviors. More often than not a simple redirection early on can prevent any confrontations and gently allow the puppy to know that you are in charge.

Example:

Your puppy discovers that shoes are great chew toys. Rather than reprimand the puppy for chewing on the shoe and in so doing possibly cause fear issues, backwardness, or resentment, simply get an acceptable toy replacement and divert (redirect) the pup's attention from the shoe to the toy. Interact while quietly removing the shoe from harm's way☺.

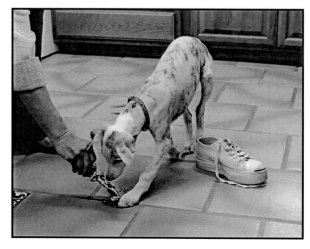

Teaching through redirection is an approach that is not only successful, but also has added benefits:

- ✦ It results in greater interaction between you and the puppy (and you are paying more attention to your dog—essential!).
- ✦ Bad habits are not learned or fostered.
- ✦ The puppy learns to come to you for all good things.
- ✦ Your puppy's focus is more concentrated on you.
- ✦ You yourself will have a more positive attitude, avoiding negative emotions such as frustration or anger.
- ✦ A stronger bond with mutual respect evolves.

So when your puppy is doing something you prefer he not do, such as sniffing or chewing or digging, don't react negatively (bad attitude), redirect. Divert his attention from the undesired behavior onto something interactive and progressive.

Redirect the unwanted behavior before it becomes a habit!

This requires that you be paying attention to what your dog is doing whenever you are together. It is your attention to your dog that will help shape and direct your dog's character and behaviors.

Attention goes both ways.
Do not ignore your dog and your dog will learn not to ignore you.

Attention is a two-way street:
It goes both ways!

1.5 MANNERS COUNT!

A well-mannered dog is one you can take anywhere and be proud. A well-mannered dog is civil at home and in public, can comfortably accompany you on walks, exhibit self-restraint upon greeting other humans or dogs, and come without hesitation when called.

Good manners demonstrate an understanding of place and respect: a dog that has good manners is a dog that is content.

1.5.1 TEACH FIRST!

REMEMBER: it is your house, your rules. For your dog to succeed in recognizing and obeying those rules, you must first teach the dog what those rules are. Again: your dog cannot second quess you nor read your mind. Teach him what you want and delight in the results!

Teaching a puppy to 'come' is generally extremely easy, as most puppies want to be with their person. The more time you take to teach your new arrival what 'come' means and that its execution results in lots of hugs and praise, the faster and more deeply ingrained your dog's response will be.

CAUTION: if you want your dog to respond to the first command you give, be sure you teach him this from the onset. If you give multiple commands like 'Come. Come. Puppy, come.', your pup is going to learn to come on the third, fourth, or even fifth call—if at all.

> *Say what you mean and mean what you say!*

So teach your young dog to respond to a first command!

Begin by using 'success' to teach: start <u>up close</u>. Puppies have a very short attention span. If you are too far away, your puppy will most likely get distracted while coming towards you. Set yourself and your new puppy up for success by staying close so that distance will not be a factor.

Call your dog with one command and one command only. You may want to move backwards in order to entice your dog to come quickly. The movement helps to draw the dog to you. The nanosecond your puppy responds to your call, praise and encourage verbally with sincerity while your pup is coming toward you. Clap your hands. Leap for delight. Make coming to you a joyous event!

Convince him that he is the best in the world—which he is! When your dog reaches you, interact! Play, ruffle him up with petting, whatever suits you best. But do make it worth his while. You want your dog to **<u>want</u>** to come long before you instill the **<u>must</u>** come. This makes the entire process much easier and more enjoyable.

Be careful that when you do call your puppy to you, you are not waving a toy to entice your new companion. Should you do so, your puppy will be responding to the toy, not to you or your call. Keep the toy hidden until your puppy reaches you, then bring it out as a reward.

Interact. Make coming to <u>you</u> something your dog understands and enjoys.

Using a food treat initially, this handler insists his puppy
'touch' him when called—this prevents flyby's

A safety precaution is to teach your dog to 'touch' you upon reaching you. All too often a dog will run back towards you when called, come near, then suddenly bolt off again without so much as a by your leave. In my estimation, this is not good enough nor is it safe. By teaching your dog to touch your hand when called, you are insuring that you will be able to seize him and hold him back for safety purposes should the need arise.

Once your dog understands what the command is, always insist that he come on the first command. Multiple commands result in options, and if you give your dog options, you are no longer in charge: he is. Naturally he is then going to do what pleases **him** most, not what pleases **you**.

1.6 TEST YOURSELF

Allow your dog to become distracted. Call him. **ONE COMMAND only!**

(Pay close attention to this and listen to yourself: many handers aren't even aware that they are giving multiple commands.) Your dog should respond promptly. If not, then you have either not taught him what the command means, OR you have unintentionally been giving multiple commands all along and your dog is taking advantage of your indecision.

If your dog has learned to ignore you when you call him, then you will need to reverse that way of thinking in him.

Put the dog back on a drag line or the like. You need to be able to control the situation. Allow the dog to wander. Once he is distracted, call him. ONCE ONLY!

If he does not respond, then simply take up the drag line and give him a light 'pop' as you back away. (Note: the 'pop' utilizes only a wrist action. Do not use the elbow or shoulder when giving these light pops. To employ the elbow or shoulder action when popping would result in a yank, not a pop. Be alert to this.)

You may encourage him with positive reinforcement, but do NOT use the call word in that encouragement. Say things like, "Thata boy! Yes for you! Etc." You want your dog to <u>want</u> to come—and only on the one command.

Once he reaches you, interact!!!! Make being together meaningful and desireable.

1.7 BASIC BEHAVIORS TO TEACH TO ESTABLISH HOME RULE

1. **EARLY SOCIALIZATION** — and this means getting your dog out into the public often and allowing him to become comfortable with the world at large — is essential for your future performance dog. You want your dog to be at ease in strange environments so that he can function to the best of his ability without undue stress or trauma. So take your dog with you as often as possible and make a pointed effort to introduce him to all sorts of places, people, and things so that he is mentally stable and adaptable.

2. **CRATE TRAIN!** You want your dog to be content to stay in a crate. The crate should be a safety zone for your dog, a place where he can go and feel secure. Never, ever reprimand your dog when he is in his crate. This is his sanctuary. A crate is also a place where he can stay when at some trial and rest. Having a crate trained dog can also be invaluable for you, as it is a place where you can keep your dog and know he is safe. The dog can relax and you can relax.

3. **A 'WAIT' OR 'STAY' IS MANDATORY.** Begin teaching this behavior early on, particularly when feeding. Begin with short successes and build on these until your dog can stay in place for 5-10 minutes. Have your dog stay when you are opening the front door so that he does not learn to bolt out. Not only is this a 'respect' issue, it is a safety net: a dog that bolts could run out in front of a car. It's happened. Have your dog stay in his crate until you give him the okay to come out: do not allow him to make a break for it the moment you open the crate door. Unacceptable! Be in charge — and play it safe.

At her very first lesson, Glimmer accepts that she must wait until given the okay.

4. "LEAVE IT" is a handy command that your dog should understand well. Chiefly 'leave it' means 'ignore that', 'don't touch it', 'don't even go there.' It can also mean 'that's not yours, it's mine.' When you tell your dog to 'leave it', your dog should pull back and desist. Knowledge of this command can be translated into many situations:

   a.) To stop your dog from eating something gross discovered while on a walk, for instance.

   b.) To break strong eye contact between your dog and another dog.

   c.) To stop your dog from rudely grabbing food or a toy from your person.

   d.) To stop your dog from rifling in your training bag or such like thing.

   e.) To stop your dog from amorous flirtations.

   f.) To stop your dog from sniffing.

These are but a few instances where a strong understanding of 'Leave it' can be put into practice. As stated earlier, it's a handy command to have at your disposal.

1.7.1 Teaching "Leave it."

1. Sit your dog.
2. Take hold of the collar—not the leash or drag line, but the collar.
3. Drop a piece of food or a toy in front of your dog.
4. Say 'Leave it' as you give the collar a light wrist pop—merely a 'check'.
5. If your dog struggles, give a second check on the collar.
6. Once your dog is accepting that he may not have the cookie or toy, release your hold on the collar.
7. Praise your dog with a quiet, soft voice (enthusiasm could cause your dog to leap for the food or toy.)
8. You pick up the toy or treat: the dog must NEVER be released to the reward.
9. You present the toy or treat to the dog. You are in charge of this reward, not the dog!

Once your dog understands that 'leave it' means that he should ignore whatever it is you are insisting he ignore, then you can begin applying the 'leave it' command to other situations.

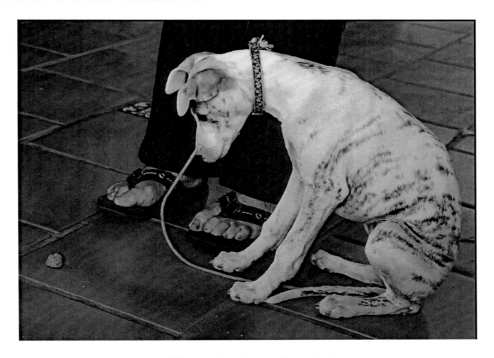

Glimmer learning to 'Leave it.'

1.8 THE BOND THAT BINDS

Spend as much time with your canine buddy as is possible. Pay attention to him.

Eye contact is enormously important. Teach your dog that eye contact is wonderful. Praise him when he looks at you—and put a name to the behavior like 'Good look' or 'Good watch'.

Learn as much about him as he will learn about you. This mutual understanding will help create the bond a team needs in order to excel.

The nurturing of your future performance puppy's character is most greatly affected between the ages of 7 weeks to 6-8 months. It is during this stage that you need to establish your position as pack leader. It is also the stage where you can most direct your young dog's interests and makeup. Take advantage of it!

There are two vital things you can do to best assist this development:

1. Spend as much quality time with your puppy as you can.
2. Spend even more time with him☺.

Spend as much quality time as you can with your canine companion. It doesn't matter what you do as long as you are interacting.

Here is what I do when a new puppy enters my household:

a. The puppy is crate trained, sleeps in a crate by my bed.

b. The puppy goes everywhere with me for optimal socialization. (Even if, at times, he must be carried for health reasons, i.e., to avoid parvo et. al.)

c. A 'puppy crib' is set up in the rec room. (The crib is basically a low x-pen placed over layers of non-toxic absorbent materials.) A few benefits this crib affords are:

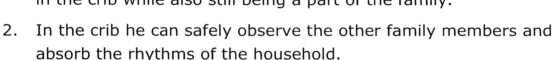

1. The puppy can move freely and securely when in the crib while also still being a part of the family.

2. In the crib he can safely observe the other family members and absorb the rhythms of the household.

3. My other dogs can see the puppy and accept him into the fold—but there is little other interaction. I want my new puppy to focus on me, not my other dogs. It is to me that the puppy must come for food, amusement, love, fun and games, and attention, especially during those first critical 6 months of development.

4. The crib helps me keep the puppy isolated from my other dogs while in the house without penalizing my adult dogs in any way. My adult dogs have free reign.

5. The 'crib' affords me a bit of freedom too. I can talk to the puppy while moving around, hands free, and not be constantly watching the puppy to make sure he is not getting into trouble or about to have an accident. The crib is 'breaktime!'

d. Whenever my puppy is free—but only when supervised!—he wears a 'drag' line (meaning the pup drags the line, not the reverse.) so that I can easily catch him should the need arise. I have to be able to control his behaviors

Note the dragline on this puppy->

and <u>redirect</u> when necessary: the drag line acts like an arm extension, giving me a longer reach. (This dragline has no 'handle'; it is merely a straight piece of line.)

e. When I am going to be sitting or standing in one place (cooking, for example, or at my computer) for any length of time, the drag line is tied to a belt loop, affording me the opportunity to have him near and to talk to him with regular eye contact. This also teaches the puppy to be calm at times.

f. I make a point to isolate myself and the puppy 2-3 times a day and play with him. The play is indispensable in helping to develop our relationship. Additionally, many of the games we play are designed to foster certain behaviors I want him to have in our future teamwork. (see Chapter 1.8)

g. Once my puppy is old enough, I take him to performance events so that he learns to fully accept the noise, other dogs, trial smells, and the general commotion found at trials.

> When I first picked up my Cattle Dog puppy, Huckleberry, and brought him home, a friend joined me and watched as I set Huck down in the crib I'd prepared. I sat down in the crib with him and began 'playing'. My friend watched, then exclaimed, "You've started training, haven't you?"
>
> I laughed. "Sure have, but he doesn't know that. He thinks we're playing."
>
> And that's how it should be…

It's critical that the moment your puppy comes into into your household that you immediately take charge of the direction in which you want your puppy to go. This requires that you give the puppy a great deal of attention and that your attitude be upbeat and tolerant.

1.9 REDIRECT UNWANTED BEHAVIORS *NOW!*

Something to ponder: if your puppy learns to amuse himself, why would he need you as a companion or teammate? *He has himself!*

A dog that self-gratifies with self-amusement is not a dog that is going be a willing, attentive, enthusiastic partner. He will have his own stimulus; what you offer will not appeal to him.

> *Attention is a two-way street:*
> *do not ignore your dog, and your dog*
> *will not learn to ignore you.*

It is only through your attitude to training and your attention to your dog that you can instill interest and 'want to' in your dog. It's imperative that when you are with your dog, you do not ignore your dog. It's guaranteed that if you ignore your dog, you're dog is going to ignore you and subsequently learn undesirable behaviors that you probably won't even recognize until those undesirable behaviors are habits. You are, after all, ignoring your dog: there is no way you could notice the habit taking hold.

Example: Sniffing.

While training—and this means the ENTIRE time, not just when you are practicing a particular skill—**never** allow your dog to sniff. Sniffing easily becomes a habit and is very self-rewarding. Furthermore, if the dog is sniffing this means you are not paying attention to the dog. Too, if the dog is sniffing, you are no longer in charge: the dog is. In order to be a proper leader, you need to pay attention to what your dog is doing!

On those occasions when you are unable to pay attention to your dog, simply put your dog in a 'settle' so that he cannot develop undesirable behaviors, or put him in his crate where he is secure and comfortable. Avoiding the development of bad habits is easier than breaking the habit. Just pay attention.

Whenever you are in the company of your dog—especially when training—you must never allow your dog to ignore you. The more attention you give to your dog, the more attention you will receive in return.

1.10 GAMES THAT BOND

Games are a great way of engaging your dog and keeping your dog focused on you—and subsequently keeping you focused on your dog. Mutual focus is fundamental for teamwork.

On top of that, games are enormously beneficial in helping to build a strong bond between you and your dog while being extremely enjoyable!

What can possibly be more entertaining than teaching and learning through interactive games? Additionally, many games innately incorporate skills that lay a foundation for future training. Here are a few I introduce all of my dogs to:

As with everything, I will first TEACH the dog each game. I teach through SUCCESS.

So when I introduce my puppy to any of the following games, I will make darned sure that he succeeds every time and every step of the way. Only after I am sure that my pup understands the gameplan will I increase the difficulty of each game.

Remember: teach through small successes. Build your dog's understanding and confidence—and enjoy the process!

---

1. Hide and Seek

Hide and seek can be played in two different ways: the first would be to hide yourself and have the dog find you; the second would be to hide an object (toy, article, food) **on your person** and have the dog find it. In either instance it's imperative that you initially start small with either yourself or the object partially visible so that the dog can win.

   a.) Wait for your puppy to get distracted, then quickly crouch down partially (some part of you should be visible) behind a wall, tree, armchair, whatever is handy, but nearby. Say your puppy's name in a teasing fashion. Once your puppy finds you, leap for joy! Praise with great feeling and excitement. Make your puppy feel he just discovered a boneyard!

This version of hide and seek builds your dog's desire to keep one eye on you in case you decide to take off again. It's a great 'attention' builder.

b.) Take whatever object you mean to hide, show it to your puppy, then partially hide it behind you and ask him to find it. *"Where is it?" "Where'd it go?" "Where's your toy?"* If he doesn't respond, bring the toy out and tease him with it again. Partially hide it and again verbally entice him to find it. **Once he finds it, INTERACT!** Interaction is vital. Having the toy on your person is just as important: remember, all good things come from you. Finding the toy on you, followed by the interaction makes the game more thrilling and keeps the dog focused on you.

2. Toy Retrieves

All dogs have prey drive in varying degrees, which means getting a dog to run out for a tossed toy is generally very simple. It's the _bringing back_ that is the hard part. Again, first teach:

Start small. With a puppy I like to sit on the floor so that when my puppy is coming back to me he is learning to look at my face. Sitting on the ground makes me shorter and more eye-level, making it easier for my puppy to learn this eye contact during the play without his ever being aware of it. The eye contact is a side effect, but an extremely desirable one.

The puppy will be wearing his drag line. The first thing I will do is tease the pup, get him all excited about the toy, then I will lightly toss it 2-3 feet away—just beyond my feet.

Do **NOT** toss it far. Should you toss it too far, your pup may get distracted before he reaches the toy and your efforts to teach the retrieve will be fruitless. Too, if you throw it too far, you no longer have the control you need to get your puppy to return it to you. It's essential that you control the situation in order to teach. Keep the toss close so that your puppy can succeed!

Once my puppy reaches the toy I begin to happily call him back to me with the word "Bring." Because it is so close, the puppy generally does. Once he reaches me, I PLAY a bit of tugs with him. If you simply take the toy away when he brings it to you, your dog is not going to want to bring it to you very often. It's very important that once the item is returned, you interact with it with your puppy!

Now, if my puppy decides he'd rather bolt off rather than bring it to me, I simply stop him with the drag line, reach out and take hold of the toy which I then use to guide him back to me while verbally telling him what a good 'bring'.

Once he is very close I will make strong eye contact and play tugs while praising him for his 'bring'. Good bring! Yeah for you! What a good bring!

I would then repeat the entire process.

Note: remember to reel your puppy back in with the toy, not the drag line. Should you use the drag line, your puppy will most likely resist and drop the toy, perhaps even throw a small tantrum. This is counterproductive! Use the toy to 'bring' him back to you.

Many puppies will drop the toy on the way back, eager to leap into your arms. (Aren't puppies wonderful!) Should this happen, simply reach out and get the toy, wiggle it around while you entice your puppy to get it, and without letting go, once your puppy dives for it, gently guide him back into you with the toy and play with it with him. SHOW HIM how to succeed! Then build on these successes.

Patience and perserverance are required☺. Above all, enjoy the process!!!

(If you are starting out with an older dog, sit in a chair and instead of using a drag line, use a leash. Otherwise, the process is basically the same.)

3. Motivational Recalls

Almost all puppies will bound happily back to you when called. Watching a puppy run towards us with all his heart and soul is one of the things about puppies that makes us smile and feel wonderful about life. Take advantage of this eagerness and willingness to teach them to come dashing back every and any time you call them. Here's how to start:

1. Have someone hold the puppy in place.
2. You walk away, talking to your puppy, teasing him to get him excited, perhaps even showing him a toy to build his drive. Excite him so he wants to explode towards you!
3. Initially don't go more than 15-20 feet away. Remember: you want your puppy to succeed!
4. Finally turn and face your puppy, still verbally enticing him.
5. Call him—and have excitement in your voice!
6. Once the puppy indicates that he wants to respond (wriggles, tries to escape, or shows any desire whatsoever), the person restraining the puppy must let go when you call.
7. Your puppy should shoot out like a race horse out of the start gate.
8. Once your puppy reaches you, INTERACT!!!!

Play! Praise! Pamper! Play!

> ### *Always interact and make the recall a cause for celebration!*

If you do not have a second person to help, here is an alternative:

1. Toss a toy a <u>short</u> distance and have your puppy run towards it.
2. As your puppy is running for the toy, you take off (not too fast—you want your puppy to win) in the opposite direction, calling him as you go.
3. The moment you hear or recognize in any way that your puppy is getting near to you, stop running and turn to face your puppy.
4. Continue to be verbally encouraging and joyful at his response!
5. Once your puppy reaches you, **interact!**

Play! Praise! Play!

4. Marking

Basically 'marking' is teaching the dog to follow your arm direction to wherever you are pointing.

Obviously this is a behavior that can be transferred to many areas in numerous performance venues once the dog grasps the concept. By introducing your young dog to a marking game that is ultimately self-rewarding, you are not only teaching the dog to look where you are pointing, you are building up his desire to do so.

I like to use those 5" white lids from cottage cheese or yogurt containers, which I save up. The small, dessert-sized white paper plates will work just as well. Scatter these target dishes around, at least 8 feet apart. I find a large circle or half-circle works nicely. Initally work very close to the one you are going to send your dog to. Allow the dog to watch as you place a small, quickly swallowed treat on the plate.

Step back beside your dog and while holding your dog back with your right hand on his collar, hold your left arm along side his head and point to the baited target dish. Tell him to "Mark" in a teasing, excited voice. Say things like, "There's your mark. Mark it! Good mark. Yes, that's mark."

When you feel him wanting to take off for it, let him rip.

This is a game that not only builds drive, it infuses the 'want to'.

Once he's there and grabbed his goodie, call him back to you, interact (remember: you want him to be overjoyed to come back to you!), and then set up for one of the other target plates.

Start with short distances and gradually build distance as your dog improves.

You can do this with toys as well. Have your dog 'mark' a toy, then send him for it. After he brings it back, play with him. Enjoy being together!

Test Yourself

1. Have your dog sit and wait while you put his food dish down.
   Does he wait until you give the 'okay'?

2. Let your dog eat a bit, then take the dish away.
   There should be no complaints, solely compliance.

3. Tell your dog to 'sit'. Listen to yourself. Are you using one command only?

4. With your dog in a sit, drop some food or a toy at his feet as you say 'Leave it'. Again, there should be total compliance.

5. Tell your dog to stay (one command only!) and open the front door.
   Your dog should remain where he is until you give him leave to move.

6. Call your dog to you (again, only one command!) Your dog should respond immediately. You are, after all, the pack leader.

**The above are strong pointers as to who is in charge.
Remember: it must be you!**

1.11 CHAPTER REVIEW

Leadership is the first and most crucial building block when assembling a team. It's the cornerstone that supports the entire structure. YOU need to be that leader, hands down.

> ### *No leader, no team: it's that simple.*

And leadership begins at home.

Just because a dog may be trained to perform does not mean that he ultimately will. Too often I have seen a well-trained dog go into a performance arena and, to put it bluntly, utterly ignore the handler and do his own thing.

Zooming playfully around the ring is a common example. Sniffing uncontrollably—and generally in a different direction from the handler—is another case in point . And then there's the dog that leaves the arena entirely, off on a joyful fling and playing 'catch me if you can' with everyone on the grounds. He's having a lark, and enjoying the whole process.

These actions are the behaviors of a dog who does not have a leader and so has assumed the role himself. And why not? Somebody has to do it.

First and foremost, be the leader your dog needs you to be. Believe me, your dog will still love you. Even better, he will love and <u>respect</u> you.

Because a dog is a pack animal—meaning he is best adapted to living within a group—he responds best to social order. Knowing where he stands within the pecking order allows him to feel more comfortable and more secure. He will be content.

Photo by Ruth Anderson Barnett

Take charge of the direction in which you want your new dog to grow and develop. Be patient, persistent, and clear. It is your <u>attitude</u> that will impact the response and rapport that will gradually unfold as you spend time together.

Spending time together is mandatory as well. Your <u>attention</u> to your dog is directly proportional to the amount of attention you will receive in return. Additionally, you and your canine buddy will form an everlasting bond that cannot be bought in any store, reproduced in any factory, or broken by any earthly power.

Leadership: your dog needs it,
your team needs it.
Go for it!

**Good manners count, less chaos reign.
Leadership is vital!!**

Chapter 2: THE CANINE TRINITY™

What to expect in this chapter:

- What leadership means
- Sight
- Sound
- Smell
- Body language counts
- Ideas to help redirect negative emotions
- Chapter review

The wolf is a hunter. He must use all of his wits and abilities to hunt successfully. Survival depends upon it. He uses his remarkable nose to track the prey, his large ears to hear his prey even when it is under ground or under snow, and his eyes to see prey.

The dog is a direct descendent of the wolf and as such has retained many of the instincts and sensory abilities of the wolf. A dog has an extraordinary sense of smell. The dog's hearing is extremely acute. And the dog's night vision is exceptional.

Sight, sound, smell: these comprise what I like to call the **Canine Trinity™**:

THE CANINE TRINITY™

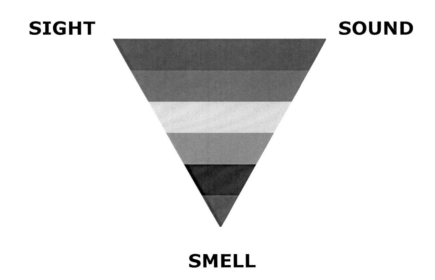

In order to better teach and work with your canine buddy, it's important to understand his needs and how he functions.

Recognizing his physical strengths and weaknesses can allow you to better guide and deal with the individual requirements and wants of your particular dog.

For example, you may want to exaggerate a jump signal to better assist your dog (visual aide). Or perhaps turn down the volume on your commands so as not to frighten your dog (audio aide). Certainly you want to do whatever is necessary to optimize your teamwork.

Know your dog's strengths and weaknesses so that you can counterbalance with your own, thereby optimizing your teamwork and performance.

It's also important to realize that the dog uses the Canine Trinity™ to assess humans, to read us. Though a descendent of the wolf, dogs have been domesticated. Most no longer have to hunt, being totally dependent upon humans for their food and shelter.

The dogs' survival and ascent among humans is directly related to their superb ability to read us and not only endure, but excel.

The relationship that has evolved between us humans and the dog is not only unique, but exquisitely beautiful.

For those who enjoy training and trialing with your dogs, awareness of the dog's capabilities as well as of what you project to the dog and how it is being received—how the dog is reading you—can help shape the teamwork as well as assist your dog's ability to learn and perform.

Attention to the Canine Trinity™ will enhance training, bolster attitude, and optimize team performance.

2.1 WHAT BIG EYES YOU HAVE!

Of the three senses—sight, sound, and smell—sight is the dog's weakest. We need to recognize this weakness and understand our dogs' visual perspective in our dealings with them so that we can best assist them when training and competing.

A dog's vision depends heavily upon movement. Dogs are exceptionally alert to motion, and in fact are able to see a moving object more than ½ mile away. Stationary objects, on the other hand, are more difficult for them to recognize, especially when the object is up close.

Reflect: have you ever entered a room where your dog is sleeping soundly and you just stand there without moving, watching them, when suddenly your dog wakes up and does NOT recognize you?

Some dogs bark, others cower, but it's evident that the dog doesn't immediately know who you are?

Often owners attribute this to the dog having just woken up and being disoriented. In truth it's because the dog does not initially recognize your shape without the movement. Once you move, the dog suddenly realizes that it's you and he becomes all happy and wiggles his way toward you. He's probably also relieved!

Shape and movement: two characteristics that heavily influence your dog's ability to see well.

Dogs can see **four times** better than humans in the dark.

As descendents of the wolf, the dog's eyesight is best adapted for night vision—which is when most animals hunt.

Like us, their retinas have both rods and cones (photoreceptors), but dogs have many more rods than we do. Rods take in light. This means dogs are able to draw in more light at night than we are, making their night vision extremely good. It's estimated that dogs only require about ¼ the amount of light that we do to see things at night. That's how good their night vision is!

Dogs have fewer cones than we do, however, and it is the cones that control color. But they do have a few cones; hence, they are not completely color-blind as many believe. Having fewer cones, they simply don't see the <u>range</u> of color that we humans have. But they can see an array of very dark grey, dark yellow or brown, light yellow, gray, light blue and dark blue.

> ## *Test Yourself:*
>
> **Sit up straight with your feet flat on the ground. Place your hands in your lap and relax. Now frown. That's right, frown. Notice that when you frown, your body deflates. Your shoulders droop, if only slightly.**
>
> **Now feign anger. Pretend you're really angry. Notice how your body grows and stiffens, becomes more rigid. Anger makes you look bigger and more aggressive.**
>
> **The OUTLINE of your body moves and shifts—if even minutely—to reflect your mood changes. Your dog is absolutely going to recognize any minor changes and respond accordingly.**

Understanding what your dog might be seeing when you are working with him can only help you to improve your training, to better assist your dog's success in his training, and through that success, have stronger teamwork.

It is your job to be alert to your own reactions and moods—to pay <u>attention</u> to what you are projecting through your body language and to have the right <u>attitude</u> so that you are constantly bolstering your dog's confidence and strengthening his drive.

> ## *So when training or trialing, be sure your attitude is POSITIVE!*

2.1.1 THINGS TO 'LOOK' OUT FOR WHEN TRAINING OR TRIALING

1. Become more aware of eye contact and how your dog might be reading you. Naturally there are times eye contact will enhance your performance, but there will be times that it can be a hinderance, even cause the dog to 'freeze'. Look at your dog. Watch him. Discover what best suits his individuality.

2. Pay attention to your facial expressions: your deep concentration could conceivably be interpreted as a scowl. Certainly there have been times when someone has asked you, "What's wrong?" and you reply, "Oh, nothing. I was just thinking."

   But consider how your dog might be reading this. He probably thinks something is wrong as well! So do be more conscious of your expression. Better yet, SMILE.

3. When nervous, you may be stiff, even rigid. Relax. Close your eyes and calm yourself with pleasant thoughts (visions of a spectacular run, for instance) so that you can project a better profile.

4. All trainers occasionally experience frustration and disappointment: be careful not to confuse your dog with these emotions, especially during a performance run. Your dog can learn to associate your being unhappy with the ring situation—<u>not</u> an association you want to foster!

   You want your dog to love performing with you! So if something causes you to be disappointed or frustrated, shelve it until after you are finished. Think of future performances and continue with style. Once calm, reconsider the situation and find a way to rectify it. There's always a solution.

5. When training or trialing, should you yourself make a mistake—give a wrong command, miscue, whatever—and in response hit your forehead with the palm of your hand (the old "Dumby me" salute), realize that your dog does not know that you are chastising yourself. *Most likely your dog will take it personally.* It could be demoralizing—certainly confusing—and consequently undermine his confidence and ability to learn. Be less reactionary and pay more attention to what the dog is seeing—and what you might be doing to your dog unwittingly!

6. Become more conscious of your slightest body movements. Dipping a shoulder, turning slightly right or left, leaning forward, bending over your dog, etc.—any and all of these can have unsuspected consequences when your dog is tuned in and reacting to the sublties of your body language.

And of course, **NEVER** exhibit anger or frustration. Being angry with your dog, the situation, a rude remark, some bad luck, or a 'stupid' judge will not only interfer with your ability to pay attention to the needs of your dog (being a good leader), it will ultimately backfire and undermine your entire performance or training time. Anger is utterly unproductive all the way around.

Body Language Counts!

2.2 WHAT BIG **EARS** YOU HAVE!

HEARING. The wolf uses his large upright ears to hunt and locate prey. He also uses them to detect danger. As a descendant of the wolf, a dog's hearing is also quite exceptional.

It's interesting to note that there is no animal in the wild that has drooping ears. The ability to hear well in the wild is far too necessary for survival. Only those animals that we humans have tampered with—some dog breeds and rabbits for example—have floppy ears. We have done this to give the animal a sweeter, more friendly appearance.

Animals in the wild aren't particularly interested in looking sweet or friendly; they're more interested in living another day. Hence, their ears have remained upright and/or enlarged.

Dogs can hear much higher frequencies than humans. This is important to recognize in our dealings with dogs—and one capitalized on in hunt work and herding: the silent dog whistle. This whistle cannot be heard by us. It is at such a high pitch that it is beyond a human's hearing range. But the dog certainly hears it. Better yet, the dog can recognize the particular whistle being blown by his owner.

Dogs can alert to their human returning home long before the family car pulls into the driveway. The dog identifies a high frequency emitted from the engine and recognizes it, so can be at the door or gate to greet you with gusto.

It's been determined that a dog can hear and identify your particular car from as far away as ONE MILE!

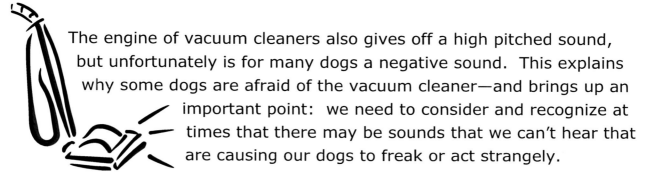

The engine of vacuum cleaners also gives off a high pitched sound, but unfortunately is for many dogs a negative sound. This explains why some dogs are afraid of the vacuum cleaner—and brings up an important point: we need to consider and recognize at times that there may be sounds that we can't hear that are causing our dogs to freak or act strangely.

We should not simply dismiss their behavior to some character flaw. Rather than saying the dog is being 'silly' or calling the dog 'cowardly', it might be better to look around and see if there is something with an engine that could be causing the dog's reaction.

We need to be open-minded as well as fair. Understanding that dogs can hear sounds well outside of our own hearing range can give us a better appreciation of them and some of their reactions that we might not otherwise comprehend.

We also need to realize that we do not have to scream at the top of our lungs in order to be heard!!

Voice plays an **_enormous_** role in training. When we speak, our dogs may not understand the words precisely, but they certainly distinguish and interpret the sound!

Try This:

In a happy, warm voice tell your dog what a bad, bad boy he is. Your dog will probably wag and be quite pleased with himself.

Now tell your dog in a harsh, ugly voice what a good, good boy he is. No doubt he's going to pull in to himself and look confused.

It's the TONE, not the words!
Now love him up! He needs reassurance☺.

Sincere praise strengthens and bonds!

Just as body language plays a significant role in training and trialing, so too does voice. When working with your canine buddy you must:

✓ **Keep a positive tone!**

✓ **Be sincere in your praise!**

✓ **Use short command words!**

✓ **Be consistent with your commands!**

✓ **Give firm, but quiet commands!**

A positive tone will encourage your dog and help him succeed. Your dog will certainly recognize the sincerity of your praise—so make it so.

Short command words will be more quickly recognized than complete sentences, and therefore will result in a faster response from your dog.

It's mandatory that you be consistent with your commands!

Inconsistency can result in confusion, as the dog will not understand what is required if multiple or different commands are given for a single skill or behavior. And certainly a quieter, though no-nonsense command will draw a better response than one screamed at the dog.

It's absolutely counterproductive to shout and try to scare or threaten your dog into performing using harsh, menacing tones: ultimately the dog will shut down, and who could blame him? Instead, try using a quieter, but steady matter of fact tone and watch your dog's attitude make a turn around.

Test Yourself:

Record your next training session.
Afterwards sit down and listen carefully to yourself.

- ✓ **Are you using a positive tone?**
- ✓ **Do you hear frustration, even anger, in your voice?**
- ✓ **Are you giving multiple commands?**
- ✓ **Are you praising, and if so, is the praise sincere?**
- ✓ **How loud is your voice?**
- ✓ **Is your tone harsh, pleading, bolstering or enabling?**

Listen and grow and become the team leader your dog needs you to be.

Your **attitude** will be reflected in your voice: pay **attention** to how and what you are projecting and temper your emotions so that you and your dog can become the **TEAM** you are training for.

2.3 WHAT A BIG NOSE YOU HAVE!

Smell is the dog's keenest sensory organ. I've read that the dog's sense of smell is more than a 1000 times stronger than ours. (Compared to the human's measly 5 million olfactory receptors, a dog has 220 million!)

Dogs are now being used to detect and locate everything from termites to illegal drugs to disaster survivors, as demonstrated after the attack on the World Trade Center in 2001.

In Guam Parson Russells have been trained to sniff out the destructive brown tree snake in airports so that it doesn't get taken off the island to invade other lands. Beagles are being used to smell out agricultural contraband—prohibited foods—at international borders. The use of the dog's extremely acute sense of smell is being used in more and more ways all the time: bomb detection, locating cadavers, underground gas leaks, even cancer detection.

It has been established that a dog can detect and alert a person suffering from epilepsy that they are going to have a seizure long before it is going to happen, thereby allowing the person to prepare for it and get off the ladder or pull off the road, etc. Imagine. The dog can actually smell the chemical changes occurring in the body.

Health authorities around the world are now training "seizure alert" or "seizure response" dogs, the response being to press a button on a phone for emergency service to call for help.

And yes, dogs do react in different ways to different smells. For example, it has been determined that lavender can actually have a relaxing affect, while peppermint is more stimulating to them.

A dog's sense of smell makes them exquisitely suited for tracking. Just as every human has a unique set of fingerprints, so does each and every human have a unique smell. Tracking is one of the most natural performance venues a dog can be asked to compete in. Not only do dogs track for search and rescue—sometimes over great distances—they can do so on land or in water. Phenomenal. Truly phenomenal.

It's no wonder our dogs can read us so magnificently.

So yes, dogs can most assuredly smell fear. And anger. Depression. Joy. I like to say that our dogs probably know how we feel long before we do ourselves.

2.3.1 IDEAS TO REDIRECT NEGATIVE EMOTIONS

Controlling emotions is not easy, certainly. But when training or trialing we all need to make a concerted effort to reduce the intensity of negative feelings in order to be a better leader and teammate for our dogs. Because of the Canine Trinity™, dogs are more highly reactive to their handler's emotions and the environs than is realized. Be ever alert to this!

SIGHT, SOUND, & SMELL: you need to be aware of how your particular dog will react to trial environs, what you can do best to acclimate him, as well as learn to temper your emotions so as not to upset your teammate.

Here are a few ways to redirect your fears into excitement, your insecurities into confidence, and your inexperience into determination:

1. **GO FOR A WALK**: if you are unhappy, upset, scared, or simply feeling raunchy, do not train. These feelings will go right down the leash. "Going down the leash" means your dog is reading your mood. He's a pro at reading you! The Canine Trinity™ gives him all the equipment he needs to be a pro.

   Instead, go for a walk with your dog. The calm, soothing exercise will take you out of yourself and help to make the world a brighter place. Once you are feeling more upbeat, train. It will go a whole lot better!

   Remember: your dog has learned to read you through his senses. He can read your body language, hear subtleties in your voice that tell him how you are feeling, and he absolutely can smell your chemistry and from experience understand your mood and well-being.

   At a trial I often take a walk, sometimes with and sometimes without a dog. It gives me the opportunity to collect my thoughts and focus, while also reducing any nerves I may be having prior to competing.

2. **TRUST YOUR CANINE COMPANION:** If you are not convinced that your canine buddy can perform *to your satisfaction*, then don't enter a trial until you trust that he can. Train more. Be sure that your dog understands what you are asking. It's imperative that you believe in him.

   Once you believe, you as the team leader will be able to perform to the best of your capabilities. You will be freed from worry. You will also be free to focus on the moment: your posture will be correct, your moves will be right on, and your pace will be enthusiastic.

   You will be projecting positive body language, confident body language. This, in turn, will greatly enhance your dog's ability to focus and perform confidently. Your assurance—which he can read through his extraordinary senses of sight, sound, and smell--will give him assurance.

3. **TRAIN FOR MORE THAN WILL BE REQUIRED:** Push the limits of your training far beyond that which you would need to accomplish your goals.

   > Examples: If your dog will need to do a 40' go-out in obedience, make sure that in practice he is able to perform a 100' go-out. In agility if your dog will need to do 12 weave poles, be sure in practice he is able to do them from every possible approach and angle...with SPEED! Overemphasize! Exaggerate!

   You'll have greater success in a stressful situation when the requirements are less challenging than those you demand from yourself and your dog in your training.

   In other words, what you will need to do when performing should ultimately be less demanding than what you practice when training.

   This contrast can greatly enhance your confidence and subsequently make you less nervous, less jittery. If you are nervous and worried, your dog will know; if you are confident and strong, your dog will know. Remember: he's a pro at reading you. The Canine Trinity™ makes him one!

4. **PROOF WITH REALISTIC DISTRACTIONS:** It is very important that you introduce your dog to trial environs early in his life; it is also essential that you teach him that he can/will work comfortably and reliably in these circumstances.

Simulate potential distractions in your training regimen. For example, work your dog around other dogs being trained. Practice while someone is playing with their dog off to the side—something that often is seen at performance venues!

Introduce your dog to different sounds he may encounter when trialing (applause, riotous jubilation, another handler screaming commands, canopies going up or down, booming loudspeakers, frenzied barking.) Get your dog accustomed to the audible distractions as well as the physical. Be inventive!

Sight, sound, and smell: the Canine Trinity™. It is your duty to make sure your dog can readily accept the sights, sounds and smells associated with the competition you are performing so that he can be comfortable and so concentrate on being your team partner.

5. **ATTEND MANY PRACTICE EVENTS:** What you want to do is replicate trial conditions as near as possible — in and out of the arena. Your canine buddy needs to become comfortable working in a show-like

environment, and the simulated ambiance at practice events will contribute greatly to this end. When at a practice event, *set yourself up*.

By this I mean speak to whoever is going to take you through your paces and ask that person to tell you when something is not correct (missed a contact, crooked front or finish, etc). Get an outside commentary/opinion. Practice events give you an overview of where you are in your training. This is priceless knowledge!

It's also an excellent use of the venue—you will get a better idea of what you need to work on—and getting a verbal blow by blow will increase your anxiety. This is important as it gives you the opportunity to learn how to deal with your unease in a positive fashion.

Do not allow yourself to become frazzled, do not allow yourself to become embarrassed: focus on your dog and be there for him! Learn from the experience—and grow. In doing so you will learn greater self-control so that in a true competition you will be able to lessen your fear and trepidation and so not send out the wrong vibrations to your dog.

YOU need to make things as smooth and positive as you can so that your dog does not fret or become alarmed because of the emotional odors and signals you might be giving off.

In addition to this, you should ask friends, colleagues, and/or family to stand ringside while you are performing. This will:

a.) put more pressure on you and so subsequently better simulate a true show, and

b.) provide realistic distractions for your dog.

People often stand ringside, erect, quiet, and staring directly at you. This is a posture that is frequently intimidating to a dog. It's necessary to condition your dog to such diversions. Maintaining his focused attention on you and his job will greatly offset such distractions.

The use of practice events will also allow you to better grasp your dog's weaknesses and strengths. Knowing them (and believe me: no dog is perfect. All dogs have strengths and weaknesses!) will afford you great flexibility: you as the handler can call upon and exaggerate the strengths while working to reduce circumstances that would show his weaker areas. This takes experience, but it can be and is done.

Use matches and the like to teach you how to get started! Additionally, the practice at these venues will further acclimate your dog to the sensory bombardment he will get at an actual trial. These practice events will help condition him and strengthen his ability to function when competing.

6. **HAVE YOURSELF VIDEOTAPED:** Having someone videotape you and your canine companion going through the paces can often put things in perspective.

While being videoed you're also made self-conscious and more uneasy, which gives you the opportunity to consciously rise above these anxieties in order to focus on your job. Remember: your dog can smell your anxiety and fear. You need to learn to control these emotions.

Teach yourself to concentrate under self-imposed, apprehensive conditions and to be there for your dog, rather than to be self-conscious or worrying and fretting about what is happening outside of your teamwork.

Working at mental control during practice runs will make it easier for you to focus and be less insecure in an actual trial. You will become a stronger handler, leader.

Being videotaped also has the added benefit of allowing you to recognize what areas need work. The recording can be slowed down to isolate and study specific trouble spots as well as being watched and rewatched, giving you a valuable opportunity to evaluate and discover where you need to concentrate more in practice.

A videotape is not as effective as a match/practice event, but if you do both—have yourself videotaped at a practice event—you will double your analytical powers. You will not only learn where your training needs further work, you will develop the ability to concentrate under pressure and so give off fewer 'emissions' that might ultimately send your teammate into a tailspin.

7. **DON'T THINK ABOUT THE RIBBON: CONCENTRATE ON YOUR JOB.**
Wanting to take home a qualifying ribbon (or better) is natural. But the idea should not consume you.

This ambition should not dominate your thoughts and purpose while on the show grounds, and especially not while you're performing.

If it does, the hungry desire will actually gnaw away at your performance. This is not constructive. As a result you will neglect your part of the bargain with your dog: you won't be able to concentrate and therefore will be less than an adequate leader.

You'll be fretting and worrying and wondering if or where your dog is going to screw up in some way. This is all negative thought.

Besides being totally unproductive, this shift of your focus will cause your dog to recognize through the Canine Trinity™ that something is not right—and he will respond accordingly. You don't want the performance arena to become a negative association in your dog's mind.

Furthermore, if you aren't right there, present and attentive to your dog (and you can't be if you're worried about what *might* happen: that's the future, not the present,) there is no way you can expect your dog to be with you. A tumbling, domino effect can result, with each sequential time in the ring becoming more and more of a nightmare.

Again, you don't want being in the ring to be a place your dog wants to avoid!

You need to have the right **attitude**: you need to be positive. You must be **the leader** your dog depends upon you to be. You need to concentrate on those things that demand your **attention** and focus so that you can better assist your dog.

Concentrate on your handling, of giving the appropriate body cues, of using your voice to not only direct your dog but to assure your dog, of emitting the right vibrations (sight, sound, smell). Give inner strength to your dog rather than giving him bad vibes that his heightened senses will surely detect.

Respect your dog's physiology: be attentive to the Canine Trinity™.

8. **ARRIVE EARLY ON THE DAY OF SHOW:** You can best prepare for your performance by arriving early on the event grounds. Arriving early and setting up in a convenient, yet relatively calm place will allow your dog to acclimate and accept the sights, sounds and smells—the "Canine Trinity™"—permeating the show site that day.

It will also afford you time to work your dog a bit if desired, to assure the dog that he CAN work in this new arena. You will also have the luxury of watching the way your judge handles the ring and build a strategy based on the ring layout, etc. You'll be able to leisurely potty your dog, even play with him.

Don't arrive late, rush up to your entry point and go in unprepared. This will result in a less than desired performance no matter what level you're striving for. Nor will the experience be enjoyable—and it should be. This competition is something you have worked long and hard for. Enjoy it!

Give yourself ample time to conclude all your busy work, greet friends, warm up your dog, and relax. Calm yourself, gather your thoughts, project strength and leadership for your canine partner.

This approach will afford you the luxury of being in control. Being in control means you won't be flustered, overly-anxious or entering the ring and simply leaving your performance to chance. It will also allow your dog to have accepted the sights, sounds, and smells and so be more comfortable. In turn, he will be better able to perform.

9. **KNOW THE ORDER/COURSE BEFORE ENTERING THE RING:** Never, but never enter a ring without knowing the course or ring pattern! To do so is to leave your performance to chance, which means you will not be in control. Sure, you might get through it well enough, but it will not have the smoothness, fluidity, speed, and teamwork that it could have were you familiar with the sequence.

Don't be caught unawares by a call you aren't expecting and so are unprepared for. Have the right **attitude**: be prepared for every eventuality. Don't be caught off guard!

Knowing the course/ring pattern frees you. You do not need to focus all of your **attentions** on the signs or strain to hear what the judge is calling, you merely need to catch the visual or audible cue in order to perform. This gives you the invaluable ability to be there with your dog, to be attentive and focused and give your dog the direction and confidence he needs.

You can be the team leader he expects, not an intermediary between the judge, course, and him. This, in turn, will give you more confidence and control, both of which will greatly enhance your dog's confidence and ability to better respond to your directives.

Should you be thrown off by something you aren't prepared for, you will most likely become flummoxed, which in turn will 'go right down that leash'. Your dog will realize something is wrong. What you emit and project directly affects your dog's response levels.

> **Always Consider The Canine Trinity™ and Remember:**
>
> *Your Dog Can Read You Better Than YOU Can Read You!*

10. **VISUALIZE YOUR PERFORMANCE**: Now that you know what you will be doing in your class, have maybe even practiced some parts, take a breather. Sit down quietly and close your eyes. Mentally picture you and your dog performing together, not just vaguely, but clearly, precisely, step by step. Be positive. Feel its flow.

By clearing your mind of everything save the visual imagery of the performance you are envisioning, you will discover that you will have relaxed. Your breathing will become calmer and you will be more serene overall.

The better you understand your job as team leader, the less anxious and tense you will be. Anxiety and tension are emotions your dog can readily read. By eliminating these nervous responses —or at the very least toning them down—you will be easing the worrisome smells your dog would pick up on.

Thinking about a positive performance (and forgetting all concerns about potential disasters or NQs,) will move you toward being focused and in control—being a leader. This, in turn, will dramatically reduce your giving off negative or detrimental cues and smells to your canine partner. Again, consider the Canine Trinity™ and how you can best help your partner succeed.

11. **TRIAL AS OFTEN AS YOU CAN:** The more often you enter a trial, the more confident and knowledgeable you will become. Your fellow teammates, friends, instructor, and trainer can talk to you about performing until they're blue in the face, but the bottom line is you won't truly understand and appreciate the subtleties of trialing until you've stepped into a ring many, many times.

Like the dog, a handler, too, must become seasoned. Entering a performance arena repeatedly will give you an intuitive understanding and perception that I personally believe is individualistic: no two people understand or feel it exactly the same.

> ### *There Is No Substitute For Experience!*

Grow with the experience and learn to channel nervous energies such as anxiety and worry into positive energies such as self-assurance and self-control.

Being excited is one thing: being a nervous wreck is another. To go into a ring as tense and rigid as a lightning rod can't be fun—and it certainly won't be for the dog if his team leader is shaking and quaking and smelling of terror.

Make the journey exciting and upbeat: learn to channel your nerves into positive energies so that when you are performing you both can enjoy the adventure and look forward to more.

Huckleberry: his trust was absolute

Sight, Sound, Smell:
Body language, voice changes, and certainly smells can adversely affect a performance and a dog's reaction to showing. Become more aware of your dog's needs, responses, and effects the Canine Trinity™ can have on him. Learn to control your own emotions to best assist your dog's well-being.

HUCKLEBERRY 1998-2011

Huckleberry followed me 'blindly', even through streams and up stairs.

Absolute trust.

Between the ages of 4 & 5 my Cattle Dog, Huckleberry, started to go blind (Progressive Retinal Atrophy—today thankfully parents can be tested for this genetic disorder before being bred.)

When I realized he would be blind, I began to teach him new words, such as 'step' and 'easy', things I thought might prove helpful once he became totally blind. Being still young, he was quite active and still wanted to play. Two of his favorite activities were hiking with us and playing ball.

As Huckleberry's eyesight became more and more diminished, his enthusiasm for life remained ever high and happy, and the idea of limiting him just because he was blind broke my heart. So we never stopped playing ball, never stopped hiking. And here is what Huckleberry taught me:

> **That he could still enjoy life and do those things he loved to do despite his disability.**
> **It was all about heart.**

He would retrieve a ball by first listening to the projection/direction of my voice as I would tell him to 'go,' then listen for where the ball landed. He would run at full speed towards it (and he did run—part of his trust in me), ultimately relying on smell to finally locate it. People who watched him would marvel at his drive, his ability, and his incredible trust in me.

Likewise, when we hiked (and I only leashed him if the ground was exceedingly uneven or rocky) Huckleberry would follow my scent and listen to my footsteps. When we were confronted by a stream or small rut, I would stop, wait for him, then tell him 'easy' or to 'jump' as I jumped. He never hesitated.

Huckleberry trusted me implicitly. Remembering that absolute trust—his utter reliance and faith in me—still makes me want to cry. It was a beautiful relationship that taught me much about life and about canine companionship.

> **Huck's blindness was his limitation: we optimized his life by concentrating on his strengths:**
> **his powerful sense of smell and his acute sense of sound.**
> **Neither of us ever gave up…**

2.4 CHAPTER REVIEW

Sight, Sound, and Smell: the 'Canine Trinity™'.

Awareness of these three senses and how strongly they can influence and affect a dog's understanding, behavior, and relationship with us is our responsibility as their coach, trainer, and teammate. It is our job to recognize and understand each dog's weaknesses and strengths so that we can best assist him to succeed.

It is also incumbent upon us to work towards controlling our own body language, voice and emotions so that we can bolster and promote our dog's confidence and desire and drive.

Our dogs have great awareness of us: we, too, should be more aware of their perspective and needs. Having the right **attitude** about their requirements and paying **attention** to what we are projecting can only conclude in better **TEAMWORK.**

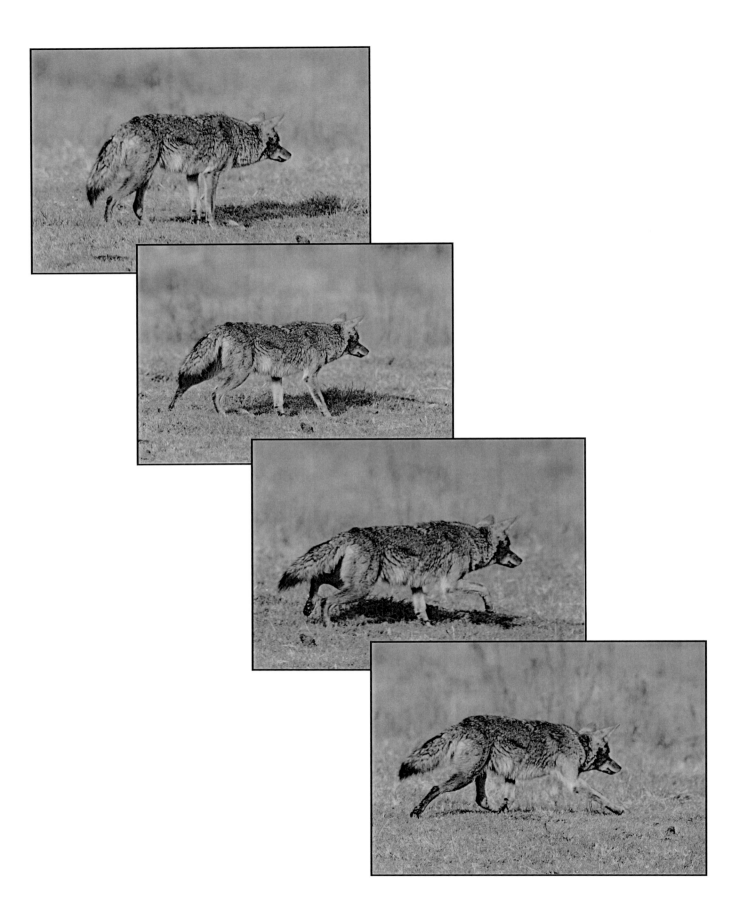

This coyote is using The Canine Trinity™ to locate its prey.

Chapter 3: THE "PERFECT PICTURE"

What to expect in this chapter:

- What leadership means
- Having a mental picture
- What the 'Perfect Picture' is
- Going through the motions
- Avoiding ruts
- Clarity in training
- Consistency in training
- Chapter review

3.1 VISUALIZING YOUR OBJECTIVE

No matter what performance venue you are undertaking—agility, obedience, rally, freestyle, whatever—you need to know where you're going. You should have a clear path to follow.

If you have a mental picture of how each specific skill should be executed as well as what you want the overall final picture to look like before you even get started, your path will be clear. You will have a destination to shoot for.

It all begins in your early training and never stops!

Before you begin teaching your dog the starting point of any particular behavior, you should break the behavior down and know:

a.) what each and every part is that will be required to accomplish the final skill or exercise, and

b.) what YOU ultimately want the performance of each of those parts to look like.

You must keep this mental picture in mind each and every time you train.

> ### *Example:*
>
> *Let's look at something simple, like the 'sit,' which is a common enough behavior across the board.*
>
> **First of all, you need to mentally determine what kind of sit you want: do you want any kind of sit, or do you want a 'tuck' sit? Is a rock-back sit acceptable? Or can it be anything as long as the dog sits? Is a puppy sit okay? Frog sit? Or do you want a tight, fast sit?**
>
> **Once you decide what it should be, you have to have the right <u>attitude</u> during your training and keep that mental picture always in mind so that every time you ask your puppy for a sit, it's a success story. Every sit will satisfy your idea of the type of sit you want in competition.**
>
> **This means you will need to pay close <u>attention</u> to every sit your puppy performs so that that 'perfect picture' of a sit becomes natural and habitual.**
>
> **Your puppy will never learn to sit any other way!**
>
> **Paying attention to the details of your idea of a perfect sit and having the right attitude when training will guarantee a solid understanding of the sit in your dog.**

3.2 WHY HAVE A "PERFECT PICTURE"?

In training it is way too easy to fall into a rut and stay there, never moving forward, making any sort of progress, or even sustaining the level you had originally achieved. Having a mental picture of what you are hoping to accomplish keeps you on the right path so that you don't end up spinning your wheels, stuck in that rut—or digging yourself even deeper.

> **Think of your training sessions as getting in a car and going for a drive: without any particular place to go, you could very easily end up going nowhere, just cruising on auto pilot—or going in circles. Certainly without a destination, you can't go anywhere because you have no idea of where 'where' is!**
>
> **However, if you get in the car and know precisely where you want to go and why, you will not only get there faster and more efficiently, you will accomplish your goal.**
>
> **So, too, is this the case when training: if you know what you want and what you want your teamwork to finally look like, you will not only get there faster and more competently, you will accomplish your goal.**
>
> **Having the "Perfect Picture" gives you a destination...**

An end point, a mental image of what you ultimately want to achieve, should be with you each and every time you train. Not only does having a *Perfect Picture* to work towards keep you moving forward, it will also help you evaluate your improvement.

You can actually measure your progress because you have something to judge it against: your *Perfect Picture.*

Having a destination and a visual image of what you want your teamwork to look like gives you the ability to immediately recognize and isolate any problems that are taking root in your training and so nip them in the bud before the problems become more deeply embedded.

Seeing the potential of a problem and not allowing it to develop is a marvelous head-start training program! This ability to stop a problem before it becomes an issue alleviates a great deal of confusion. When you take away the element of confusion, your dog can learn much faster and with more enjoyment.

> **Let's use the 'sit' example once again:**
>
> Say I picture my dog performing a pert, tight, tuck sit each time he sits. One day I notice that when I tell him to sit, he does a rock-back sit. Because I have a visual image of what I want, I know instantly that this rock-back sit is incorrect. I can immediately redirect and show my puppy how to do a proper 'tuck' sit.
>
> By being alert (paying attention) and having that perfect picture of a sit in my mind, I can stop an unwanted behavior (the rock-back sit) before it becomes an issue.
>
> Should I do nothing when I see my puppy performing a rock-back sit, then I am telling my puppy that any sit is okay—when actually it is not. In the end this attitude can only result in confusion for my puppy, especially if down the road I suddenly demand tuck sits only.
>
> Stopping the unwanted behavior before it becomes an issue avoids confusion; having the "Perfect Picture" when teaching allows me to recognize any deviations from that picture and affords me the luxury of being able to stop the glitch before it becomes a serious problem.

Without having a mental picture that you can bounce off of, you won't be able to recognize the beginnings of a problem that is creeping into your training. Suddenly the problem will just be there—and generally only realized during a performance. Something like a time bomb going off at the wrong time and wrong place.

Golden Rule:
Train to Trial!

In other words, in training never accept the picture you don't want when trialing.

Learn to pay attention to what your dog is doing when you are training. Don't just go through the motions.

3.3 WHAT DOES IT MEAN TO 'GO THROUGH THE MOTIONS'?

Say you have 20 minutes to work with your dog after a long day at the office: you take your dog and hurriedly run him through his paces, making sure to quickly cover all the skills he has been taught. The important thing is that you cover all the skills, and you do. Phew!

Here is why the above session is not productive, why it is simply 'going through the motions':

- *Time is the main consideration, not the work itself.*
- *The partnership between handler and dog is not nurtured, as time is the overall concern rather than the relationship.*
- *The quality of the workout is second to the quantity: that all the skills are covered is more important than how well they are performed.*
- *The training session lacks concentration and focus.*
- *The training session leaves little time for praise and play— essential elements to offset training rigors.*
- *Handler lacks attitude (just get through the skills) and attention (let's hurry up, we only have 20 minutes.)*
- *There is no progress in the learning curve.*
- *There is little to no teamwork.*

This makes the practice session a deception: it is not a practice session, it is merely going through a pretense of practicing.

Your training sessions should be alive (see ***Training Alive!*** ™ Chapter 6). It is healthier and more productive to concentrate on a few skills and keep them sharpened than to simply run through all your paces without attention to detail.

Be there <u>with</u> and <u>for</u> your dog. Develop the ability to see the smaller details that are a part of each skill. In doing so you will then be able to stop any departure from that *perfect picture* you are working towards.

Example:

During a practice session you tell your dog to 'down.' (Agility, Obedience, or Rally—makes no matter.) Your dog takes his good old time doing so, but finally manages to drop. This does not suit your idea of what you want, but you're thrilled your dog ultimately dropped. You may even possibly make a mental note to fix the drop later.

WRONG!

To wait, to allow this slow drop to pass unnoticed, is to mislead your dog and be unfair. The time to fix any potential problem is the moment it happens, **not** later.

In practice always show your dog exactly how to achieve the 'perfect picture' the way you wish it to be performed. Avoid confusing your dog: be clear, be consistent, be fair.

It is your job as the trainer to teach your dog how to please you, how to succeed, how to perform each exercise correctly. If you are not constant in your training, you will confuse your canine partner.

Working toward that perfect image you hold while training will put an end to confusion and greatly enhance your teamwork.

NO EXCUSES!

Example:

Your dog is working wonderfully with you, then suddenly darts off to check out something on the sideline. You call him and he comes back. You praise and continue. Your coach stops you and reads you the riot act. Your response is, "But he came back when I called him."

Your coach rolls her eyes heavenward.

That he came back is not the point. The point is that he should have never left your side to begin with!

If you accept your dog's choice to leave you during training, there is no reason in your dog's mind why he can't leave you during a performance as well.

Remember: train to trial! What you have in your training is what you will have in your performance. Don't make excuses, train to the picture you ultimately want. Always.

3.4 AVOIDING RUTS

Having a training routine is important. I highly recommend that you have a training program. However, be careful: routine can work for you or against you. Like much in life, it's a balancing act.

Routine gives order and consistency to your training, two qualities that are essential if you want to succeed. But routine can also be too convenient: it can be like wearing your favorite pair of shoes: they fit well and are extremely comfortable, but they can't be worn all the time, nor will the one pair go well with all of your outfits. You and your feet need to be able to wear different shoes for different occasions.

Breaking routine can be difficult, even disturbing. Certainly it will be unsettling—but that's the point. In order to not allow your training to become stuck in a rut with you simply spinning your wheels and getting nowhere, it is sometimes necessary to break from routine so that you can have a fresh viewpoint.

Here are three approaches you can take to help you stay on a straight course and avoid ruts:

1. Change your place of training.

Using the same training area or facility all the time is truly convenient, with multiple benefits such as affording the dog a comfortable, known environment in which to learn. Because he is secure, the dog can give more of his attention to the task you are giving him. (Remember the Canine Trinity™)

But like those old shoes, the convenience and routine of using the same training spot all the time can also have drawbacks and unforeseen consequences.

Certainly one of the results can be that the dog becomes a 'backyard wonder'—is positively perfect in the backyard or usual training facility—but is incapable of working elsewhere. Actually this is a very valid concern that every trainer needs to look at very closely.

> I, myself, have fallen victim to this syndrome. In his early days of training I thought my Dax was ready to take on the world of obedience by storm. So I took him to a match that was very well attended and entered him in the upper level classes, believing Dax would wow everyone.
>
> In Utility Directed Jumping was first. Dax did a beautiful go-out. I then gave him the bar jump. He ran to it…and stopped cold. He refused the jump.
>
> What? What the heck…?
>
> It took a couple seconds for me to take it all in, but I then quickly recognized that the bar was different from the one I used in training. This bar was bigger.
>
> Naturally I helped him succeed. We repeated the exercise and he did fine. But I was rightly humbled…
>
> To top it off, basically the same thing happened in Open, only this time with the Broad Jump. Again, the visual was different: this Broad Jump was wood and five feet wide, not the plastic four foot one Dax was used to.
>
> Believe me, the match and Dax's reactions at the event were a wonderful eye-opener for me. What I had done was trained a backyard wonder! It was now my job to break routine.

All too often you hear someone saying, "But he does it perfect at home." This is undoubtedly true. What is needed is to make sure your dog can do it perfectly elsewhere.

In order to avoid having a 'backyard wonder' that is incapable of working with any other equipment or in any other location, it is up to you to make sure you rotate training sites once your dog has grasped the concepts of what you are teaching.

2. Vary the order in which you train.

No matter where you are training, a healthy approach is to vary the order of the course or exercises you are practicing. Do not start out every practice session with the same skill. Sometimes reverse the order. Sometimes start in the middle. Mix and match.

Should you practice the same skills in the same order day after day, week after week, month after month, even year after year, you could be limiting your dog's ability to be flexible and adaptable when performing.

Teach your dog each skill/behavior, not a routine. The routine can become a habit, and this can come back to haunt you. Routine can stifle mental agility.

In most performance venues, courses and patterns and class orders will vary. Do your team a favor by preparing for this eventuality by practicing different orders in your daily training regimen. Avoid ruts. One way to do so is to change the order of exercises during training.

So for agility you might start with weave poles followed by a dog walk one day, and the next day start with a teeter followed by a tunnel. Just don't begin every training session with weave poles followed by a dog walk. Simple.

In obedience you might start with Recalls, followed by Figure 8's one day, and the next day begin with retrieves followed by the Moving Stand Exercise.

Don't be predictable or fall into a rut because of habit or convenience: randomize the order you train.

3. Modify the time of day that you train.

Another way to avoid inadvertently falling into a rut and limiting your dog's adaptability is to vary the time of day that you train.

Of course constancy and routine are important, but again, it's all a balancing act. So at some point you will need to break from the norm and inject variations. One of those variations will be to train at a different time of day.

I, personally, train in the early morning. Unfortunately, at a trial we may be required to perform in the afternoon. In order to assure that my dog is capable (doesn't balk and try to tell me that his work shift is over), it is my job to make sure that he understands that he can perform at anytime during the day. In order to do this, I need to schedule my practice times at different times. It's that easy.

So if you generally train in the evenings, occasionally work a training session in before you go to work or to do your errands. On a weekend you might want to train mid-day. Just break the mold.

Only you can implement change and be more inventive and imaginative in your training. By being flexible yourself, you are guaranteeing that your dog is flexible as well.

3.5 CLARITY IN TRAINING

Clarity is being clear. Clarity is being definite. Clarity is understanding.

Clarity in training means that nothing is ambiguous. Nothing you are teaching is indistinct or vague. Clarity eliminates confusion.

In order to avoid confusing your dog, you should always train to your *Perfect Picture.* If you are constant in your training and always training to the end results that you imagine, your dog will not only make rapid progress, but will understand how to succeed.

Certainly if you are unclear as to where you are headed, you will not be able to communicate that destination to your dog.

Clarity requires that you have a visual image to work towards. It also requires that you convey to your dog the steps required to succeed and achieve that goal.

> **For instance: if my *Perfect Picture* of "Stay" means that my dog does not move out of position at all, then should my dog anxiously scoot forward, I must indicate to him then and there that his scooting is unacceptable. The concept of "Stay" does not include a scoot!**
>
> **Sure, I'm thrilled he is so enthusiastic to get started that he can barely contain his eagerness, but should I not show him how to perform a "Stay" correctly right from the start, then I am being unfair in my training. Furthermore, down the road when he truly breaks the stay and we fail to qualify because of it, it will be my fault, not the dog's. My dog's inability to sustain the "Stay" is because early on I failed to have clarity in my training. I was not constant, I was not clear.**

With clarity added to your training, you will be able to recognize the beginnings of any blemishes to your *Perfect Picture.* Because you will have a visual image of what you want, all deviations from that picture will be more evident and so easier for you to recognize. Any and all wrong steps from what you are working towards can therefore be prevented from becoming habitual.

So what is clarity in training exactly? Let's look at another example:

In agility it's necessary that your dog understand that he must touch the yellow contacts on the various obstacles. His job is not simply to fly over the A-frame or to scramble across the teeter and leap off in order to get to the next obstacle. He must <u>understand</u> that part of the program is to touch the yellow contact.

It is your job as the trainer to spell this out for your dog in order for him to understand and to avoid any confusion.

Initially you teach him to touch the contact by showing him what is required and how to succeed. You teach a basic part of the entire skill. It is important that this concept be clear to your dog: first that touching the contact be a part of the skill, and then that it always be performed to that standard. Clarity is necessary in training this concept/skill.

Without clarity it would be utterly unfair to expect your dog to perform to your satisfaction. Without clarity your dog will *NOT KNOW HOW!*

It is your job as his trainer to *SHOW HIM HOW TO SUCCEED*, and then to sustain that level throughout his performance career.

If you have clarity in training, your dog will not be muddling about in a state of confusion. He will know exactly what is required of him. That's not to say he won't make mistakes. We all make mistakes. But he will be able to regroup and carry on without shutting down or being overly stressed.

You must pay **<u>attention</u>** to detail and have the proper **attitude** when training. Should your dog display signs of confusion, you should immediately stop and ask yourself "Have I truly shown my dog how to succeed at this? Have I been clear?"

Clarity in training will allow you to maintain the level to which you are working towards; you will be able to see and stop any unwanted behaviors immediately; most importantly, by being clear and always working towards your *Perfect Picture*, you will have a dog that understands his job and so will be much more willing to perform.

Clarity! Be clear when training: **SHOW** your dog exactly what it is you want and precisely how to succeed. It is your job to teach your dog how to perform any skill to the picture you have in mind. Again, your dog cannot read between the lines and second guess you. **YOU** must guide your dog through each minute step so that success is achieved all along the way.

Clarity in training will greatly enrich your ability to establish true teamwork: your path will be clear with your goal always in view.

3.6 CONSISTENCY IN TRAINING

It's imperative that you be consistent in your expectations and demands. Consistency! **Always** train to the visual picture you ultimately want in the ring.

If at times you insist that your dog work towards your *Perfect Picture* while at other times you accept inferior efforts, you are being inconsistent. Worse, you are going to greatly confuse your dog. Your dog cannot read your mind! Your dog only knows what you show him.

Do not simply assume your dog 'knows' what is expected or begin making excuses for responses that do not satisfy your goals. To do so will undoubtedly result in a very confused dog.

This approach to training lacks consistency. It is an attitude that is totally unfair. Consistency in training is essential.

> **Consider:** You tell your dog to go fetch the newspaper. Rover happily runs down the driveway to do so, but on the way runs over to the lawn area and grabs a ball instead. He brings you the ball. You throw it a few times while you, yourself, retrieve the paper. It's a lovely morning and all is well.
>
> The next morning you again send him for the newspaper. This time Rover sees the neighbor's dog across the way and runs over, barking his greeting. You are not happy. You stomp after him and grab his collar, chastising him by telling him that 'You know your job! You get that paper!' Tail tucked, he complies.
>
> The following morning you again send him for the newspaper. He doesn't fly down the drive. In fact he doesn't show any interest at all. What's he up to? He seems to be slinking back into the house. What the heck...?
>
> Inconsistency in having Rover fetch the newspaper has resulted in Rover's shutting down. He is confused.
>
> One of the ways a dog can tell us he is confused is by shutting down.

Consistency requires that you pay attention to detail when training. With the *Perfect Picture* before you—your end point, your goal—you must constantly be teaching and later fine tuning all the details involved so that your dog can:
    a) understand what is required and
    b) know how to do it.

Stay on your path: keep your destination in mind each and every time you work with your dog. Don't confuse your dog by allowing him to run amok along the way and then later expect him to understand that he must stay on the path with you at all times.

As his trainer, as his leader, as his teammate it is up to you to make sure he knows how to succeed. Consistency is a major factor towards that end.

Ch. OTCH Trumagik Step Aside, UDX20, OGM

One time in training I noticed that my Border Collie, Kyle, had taken a few extra steps before dropping on his Drop on Recall. Because his drop was usually right on, I did nothing. That weekend during a trial Kyle traveled considerably while performing the Drop on Recall. I was aghast—but quickly realized that this departure from my *'Perfect Picture'* was my fault: I had failed to let him know during training that this action was not desirable. Unless I let him know what is and what isn't desired, he has no way of knowing. Kyle cannot read my mind! The point deduction we received that day was due to my lack of consistency during training when I did not show Kyle that I didn't like his traveling. I was inconsistent. It was as simple as that.

The absence of consistency and clarity will cause profound confusion in your dog, and ultimately a meltdown and shutdown. You must have a forward **attitude** and pay particular **attention** to the needs of your dog. These include consistency, clarity—and fairness.

3.7 CHAPTER REVIEW

Whenever you are training, you should ALWAYS train towards a *Perfect Picture* of what you ultimately want each skill, behavior, exercise or end product to look like. Having that visual image in your mind when training allows you to:

P
E
R
F
E
C
T

- ✓ **Have a visual gauge to work against.**
- ✓ **Have a goal to work towards.**
- ✓ **Constantly be moving forward in your training.**
- ✓ **Stay on the right path and not get stuck in a rut.**
- ✓ **Have quality training sessions.**
- ✓ **Establish more consistency and clarity in your training.**
- ✓ **Become a better trainer and handler.**

Having the **Perfect Picture** when training keeps you honest: there are no excuses and no back-peddling; more importantly, a deeper understanding will develop between you and your dog.

Kyle being awarded his UDX 20 and a High Combined!

Photo by Rich Bergman

CHAPTER 4: PRAISE... AND ERRANT PRAISE

What to expect in this chapter:

- Praise defined
- Learn to listen
- Lure vs. reward
- Interaction required
- Bribe vs. reward
- 4-stage release
- Misplaced praise
- Chapter review

4.1 PRAISE IS ESSENTIAL!

I believe in praising my dog. I praise often and with great feeling. I praise from the depths of my heart. It is my contention that my sincere praise is what makes training sessions so immeasurably enjoyable for both my dog and me.

It is also my firm belief that it is this praise that infuses desire—the 'want to'—in my dog.

Without praise it's certainly possible to train a dog for almost anything. Praise is not entirely necessary to teach a dog a job. However, if I want the dog to enjoy what he's doing, to want to be with me, to be my teammate, and to perform to the best of his ability, then praise is absolutely and unequivocally mandatory.

4.2 WHAT IS PRAISE?

Praise is an expression of approval!

Given that you are the pack leader, your dog is going to <u>want</u> to please you. The more your dog pleases you, the more attention the dog gets in return. And let's face it: that's highly rewarding to the dog!

(Naturally if you are not the pack leader [see Chapter 1], then the dog will be expecting you to please him—not a healthy human/canine relationship, and an impossible relationship if you are hoping to have a performance dog.)

Fortunately your dog does want to please you. This desire in dogs is one of the many reasons why we are so enamored by them.

Their feelings for us are unqualified.

By this I mean that their feelings are pure. Their feelings do not come with limits, restrictions, or have exceptions. There are no ifs, ands, or buts.

Praise is a vital component towards a solid partnership with your dog. Praise is an expression of approval. When you praise your dog you are letting him know that you very much like what he is doing. This not only bolster's your dog's ego, it builds self-assurance, drive, and understanding.

Praise is the best reward you can possibly give your dog!

Remember that your dog has a natural desire to please you. Your approval—your praise—will amplify this desire. When your dog is happy and wants to please you, not only will his ability to learn be wide open and favorably receptive, he will WANT to learn so that he can please you even more! It becomes a cycle that makes training exhilarating.

Praise Should Be Your Dog's PRIMARY REWARD!

4.3 LEARN TO LISTEN TO YOURSELF

Are you really projecting the pride and pleasure you are feeling as you watch your dog learn?

Or do you simply mumble the praise with every footfall, "Good job. Good job. Good job. Good job. Good job."

Wow. What a yawn.

I've heard people praise their dogs like this a zillion times. It bores me to tears and is no doubt putting the dog to sleep through sound hypnosis.

"Good job, good job, good job, good job"—the mantra of dog trainers. This praise mantra lacks expression, energy, sincerity, joy. It becomes background noise that is barely acknowledged.

Remember the 'Canine Trinity™': sight, smell, sound? The dog has an extraordinary ability to read you, to understand your body language, determine your health, identify your moods, emotions…and yes, sincerity.

A person who is using a praise mantra is not infusing life into the training. On the contrary, life is being sucked out of the training.

You are simply giving your dog lip-service, which is meaningless and can actually be a real turn-off.

Praise must have meaning. Praise must be sincere. Praise should be inspiring for BOTH the trainer and the dog! And your dog, more than anyone else, will know if you mean it or not.

> *Praise must be sincere!*
> *NO mantras…*
> *NO lip-service…*
> *NO turn-offs!*

Genuine praise (fantastic **ATTITUDE**) means that you are actually focusing on your dog (you are paying **ATTENTION!**) and are truly **with** him as he executes whatever skill you are working on. You are now well on your way to establishing **TEAMWORK**.

4.4 LURE VS. REWARD

Food and toys are viable training lures. I use copious amounts of food to teach my dog. However, as soon as I can, I remove this teaching lure and replace it with tons of praise. Praise is my PRIMARY REWARD.

In my training program praise never goes away. Praise is my primary reward and is a permanent ingredient. Once I see that my dog has grasped the concept of whatever I am teaching, the lure is taken away. Food and/or toys are no longer visible.

Yes, food and toys are still an active part of daily training, but:

1) They are not visible.
2) They are used less frequently.
3) They are given randomly.
4) They are given only **AFTER** the skill/exercise is completed successfully.
5) They are no longer a lure, but a reward.

Here the toy is hidden behind...

Food and/or interactive play are a *secondary* reward and are *randomly* offered for a job well done. My dog is no longer **lured**, but **rewarded** afterwards for his success.

> *Use a LURE to teach:*
> *REWARD a learned behavior.*

A lure is like the proverbial carrot before the donkey, leading the donkey into the desired behavior. I believe in teaching through success. When teaching, the lure helps my dog succeed and so learn. It is because my dog succeeds that he learns—and more importantly, understands and so enjoys the process.

A lure is used to teach this puppy a proper tuck sit.

Once my dog understands the concept—the basis—of the skill I am introducing, the lure is removed.

A lure is used solely to teach your dog how to accomplish what you are training. The dog follows the lure into the desired behavior and so succeeds.

Teach through SUCCESS!

Once the dog has been taught the concept of any given behavior, then the lure is quickly removed. You want your dog to perform through an understanding of his job and with a desire to actually do the work.

If the lure is not removed, it is highly unlikely that the dog will ever understand what he is doing or have any desire to please you: he will only work for the lure.

A reward is given as recompense for a job well done. But realize that the job is done. The reward comes at the end of the desired behavior.

Remember...

- ✓ A reward is a prize to create <u>INCENTIVE</u>.
- ✓ A reward <u>MOTIVATES</u> your dog.
- ✓ A reward is <u>ENCOURAGEMENT</u>.

PRAISE should be your PRIMARY REWARD!

To Repeat...

LURE to teach:

REWARD a learned behavior.*

4.5 REWARD WITH INTERACTION

Jennifer and Libbey interact after the retrieve

Your dog should always come 'into' you for his reward. Interaction is mandatory!

If you simply throw out a toy or ball for your dog to retrieve, the toy or ball becomes the high point, not you. Yes, do throw that toy out, but once your dog brings it back to you, INTERACT!

You must be your dog's primary reward! If you do not praise, if you do not interact, your dog will have no reason to perform. Only you can develop that working relationship.

Your dog is not a tool at the end of a leash, purchased to do your bidding.

A dog is a living, responsive, sentient being that most certainly wants to be your partner, your companion, your teammate: you have to meet him half way.

Louise has Riggley jump up to receive his food reward.

Interaction must also apply when using a food reward: do not simply toss food at your dog, or worse, just hand it to him!

Should you merely hand food to your dog it will quickly lose its value. It will be expected—as in demanded—but it will not contribute to your dog's work ethic nor to your overall relationship.

Reinforce your leadership position with your dog: have your dog come 'into' you to receive the food.

Remember...
In your dog's world, all good things come from you!

Sincere praise is an enormous reward! Don't underestimate the value of your praise. Try it. It's grand fun all around.

4.6 BRIBE VS. REWARD

Food rewards are perhaps too easy. I love food rewards, don't get me wrong. I use food liberally to reward my dogs. But because dogs respond so readily and easily to a food reward, many people neglect to distinguish between using the food as a reward and using it to bribe their dog into performing.

The difference is in the approach...

A bribe is used to influence or persuade your dog to do whatever it is you are asking him to do. It's the lure taken to extremes. It's a pay-off.

A reward is a prize given for a job well done. It's a motivator.

*A bribe is used to get the job done:
a reward is given for a job well done!*

Bribery undermines the development of any work ethic in your dog. If you rely on bribery to train, it's unlikely that you will have a reliable, willing, and capable teammate.

Remember: your dog should be looking to you for all good things, not the reverse. Bribing is begging. When you beg your dog to perform, you are relinquishing your leadership position—and without a leader there is no team.

Example of Bribe vs. Reward:

Again let's look at the sit, that universal skill all puppies are taught:

You tell your 'trained' dog to 'sit.' Your dog just looks at you blankly, then begins to sniff around the ground. You whip out a treat and draw your dog's attention back on you, then continue to use the treat to get your dog to sit.

This is a flagrant case of BRIBERY!

Note: without the treat the dog actually ignores you. Only the presentation of a bribe persuades the dog to grudgingly comply.

Conversely, you tell your dog to sit and again he does not sit. Instead of whipping out a treat you reach down and give his collar a slight check. He sits. You stand him and again tell him to sit. This time he readily sits, eyes bright and all attention.

You verbally praise him (primary reward!), then pull a toy or treat out and interact. Interaction fuses the bond your praise is developing.

This is a REWARD!

Rewarding your dog for a job well done stimulates, encourages, and builds **attitude.** Rewards also develop your dog's confidence. Most importantly, through 'rewards' a dog learns to work for you and with you rather than for a treat. Rewards go far in developing **teamwork.**

4.7 FOUR STAGE RELEASE

It's essential that your dog be praised: this is established. But it is also vital that your dog understand **WHY** he is being praised. Understanding why will exponentially increase his ability to understand and learn. Additionally, once praised and given a reward, interaction shouldn't stop there: continued communication should follow.

It's very important that once rewarded, your dog is not suddenly stranded, ignored, and left to entertain himself.

A dog that is left dangling at the end of a leash is a dog that will amuse himself by sniffing, investigating the world, and marking. These are three common behaviors dogs readily adopt when left to their own devices. Not good☹.

In order to avoid such a disastrous outcome, adopt this 4-stage release program each and every time you wish to praise your dog for a job well done:

① Isolating the behavior that you wish to applaud can be done by **immediately** stopping in place the very instant any behavior is accomplished to your satisfaction. Simply stop.

Stopping the nanosecond your dog executes the behavior you want to praise—even if it's mid-stride—singles out and identifies for him exactly why he is being praised. The behavior is isolated. The behavior is marked.

This identification enormously assists your dog's ability to learn the skill and understand what it is you are asking of him. Through this understanding your dog will be confident and more versatile. He will have the foundations upon which to grow.

By immediately stopping when your dog has accomplished a particular skill that you wish to praise, you are **highlighting** that behavior for him. It becomes clear. It becomes specific. It can be better understood.

However, should you continue beyond the skill you wish to praise before giving any praise, this delayed praise will become too general. It becomes 'umbrella' praise covering everything—good and bad—rather than being specific and marking the precise skill you are meaning to praise.

Though still beneficial, delayed praise is not as productive in the long run as praising the **exact** behavior as soon as it happens so that the praise is very pointed, very meaningful, and has consequence: your dog will know WHY he is being praised and so will want to repeat it again to earn yet more of your praise.

Stopping at that point where your dog is doing precisely what you want him to do isolates that particular behavior and is enormously valuable towards his learning development: it clarifies!

So that's the first step: STOP!

Next you will verbally praise your dog. This is your **PRIMARY REWARD!**

Once I have stopped at that point where I am pleased with my dog's response, I let him know it. I praise!

Not only do I praise, I let my dog know what I am praising. It is my belief that dogs are more intelligent than is presently recognized. With that in mind when I verbally praise my dog, I praise and incorporate the word for the skill or behavior I'm praising into my praise:

Example: "Good sit!" "Good over!" "Good teeter!" "Good tunnel!" "Good down!" "Good look!"

I do NOT use the generic "Good job" for anything. "Good job" is too nonspecific. I want my dog to immediately recognize precisely what I am praising!

By repeating the skill word in my praise I am telling the dog specifically what it is that I am praising him for. Furthermore, by repeating the word, I am also teaching my dog that word.

Repetition is a strategic part of the teaching process!

So not only am I isolating (stopping) and then targeting my praise to a specific skill by incorporating the skill command into my praise , I am also repeating the word/command for that skill and in doing so am making the skill and praise more defined. I am teaching.

And that's the second step: VERBAL PRAISE!

 After I tell my dog how super he is doing (my verbal praise and primary reward), I will then release him upward and into me for a secondary reward.

This secondary reward can be a toy, a treat, some sort of interactive play with my person, or a combination of all three. Personally I like to vary the reward.

It's very easy to fall into a routine and so allow your training to become monotonous. Though routine is comfortable, it's not particularly stimulating. In order to keep the reward and my interaction with my dog continually vibrant, I work at not being predictable.

More importantly, it's psychologically imperative that you have the dog come into you for this secondary reward. Do NOT simply hand him a treat or toss him a toy so that he can run off and amuse himself.

By having the dog lift upwards (even if it's only to raise his front paws slightly off the ground) and come into you for his reward makes the reward more valuable and reinforces your leadership position. You control the reward. Furthermore, your dog knows that you are the one doling out that reward.

Remember:
All good things come from you!

Interactive play can also be this secondary reward which actually results in keeping the dog's attention expressly on you—not a bad thing☺. You needn't rely entirely at spitting treats at your dog.

Be more creative. Be more 'into' the whole praise/reward process. Have a truly sincere **attitude** when praising and rewarding. Pay **attention**: make sure your dog understands that the reward is coming from you and make it as interactive as possible.

And that's step three: REWARD!

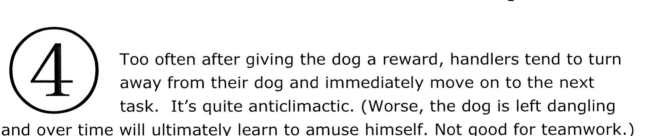

④ Too often after giving the dog a reward, handlers tend to turn away from their dog and immediately move on to the next task. It's quite anticlimactic. (Worse, the dog is left dangling and over time will ultimately learn to amuse himself. Not good for teamwork.)

Because the food/toy reward is the last thing the dog receives before being ignored—if only momentarily—then from the dog's perspective that food/toy reward will eventually become the primary rather than secondary reward.

To avoid this consequence I have introduced a fourth step into this release program, which involves **physically** praising the dog.

That's right: **PET YOUR DOG!**

After rewarding your dog with a treat or toy or hand touches or the like, immediately pet him—physical hands-on treatment—while telling him how wonderful he is and how smart he is and just what a great dog he is in general.

Pet him. Ruffle him up. Love him.

This physical interaction will keep you focused on your dog and your dog focused on you. Neither you nor your dog will learn to ignore one another, nor will your dog have the opportunity to learn unwanted behaviors while working with you. Being with you will be more important.

Additionally, this physical interaction reinforces your position as being the primary reward.

Making Step Four: HANDS ON PRAISE!

I find that this *Four Stage Release Program* helps the handler stay focused on the dog while greatly assisting the dog's ability to understand and learn.

It's a valuable teaching aide, as it helps both the trainer and dog zero in on particular skills while using very positive reinforcement to help the dog learn and even more importantly, be proud of himself.

The handler learns to pay better **attention** to training details and have a more positive **attitude**. As a consequence the dog develops a very upbeat, 'want to' attitude and has greater attention. It's a win/win situation.

FOUR STAGE RELEASE:

1. **STOP:** in order to better clarify the moment and the exact skill or response being praised

2. **PRAISE:** immediately mark the behavior with a verbal 'yes' or 'good' or the like. Then incorporate the command word in with the praise.

3. **REWARD:** release your dog to a toy, food, or some sort of interactive play. Always bring the dog into you. Relate with your dog.

4. **HANDS ON PRAISE:** physically praise your dog with great enthusiasm. Pet him, love him up while simultaneously telling him what a great dog he is!

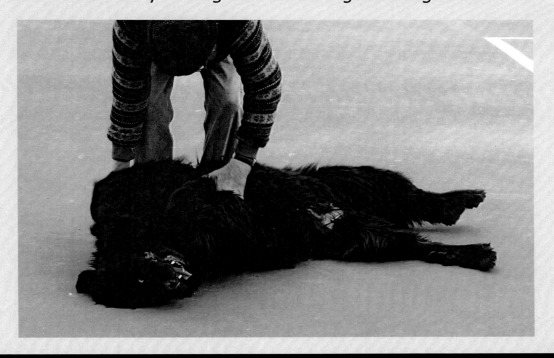

4.8 ERRANT PRAISE

Praise must certainly be sincere, that is established. But it also must be used appropriately, which means it should be given effectively at the proper time and for a reason that is clear to the dog.

All too frequently I see people praising their dog—which in itself is great—but with praise that is often unfounded and inaccurate, even hollow. It will be given for the wrong reason and/or at the wrong time and so is often misleading for the dog. This type of praise can only result in ultimately confusing the dog.

"I thought you said you liked what I was doing? Why the sudden change of heart?"

'Errant Praise' can be broken down into three categories:

1. Blanket praise
2. Praising inaccuracies
3. Misplaced praise

4.8.1 BLANKET PRAISE

Blanket praise is praise that covers everything the dog does prior to being praised. It relates to no one action, no one behavior. It includes everything—including the unwanted behaviors.

This type of praise does not clarify. This type of praise does not help the dog understand. This type of praise does not promote learning. What this type of praise does in the end is create a great deal of confusion.

> ### *Example of Blanket Praise:*
>
> **I want to work on my dog's jumping technique and confidence, so I set a series of jumps out in a long line at different heights and different intervals. However, once my dog begins going through this channel, he suddenly decides to run over to another dog, then to run zoomies around the jumps, then falls back into the setup and does a couple more jumps for me. I praise him copiously for performing these last few jumps.**
>
> **This is 'blanket praise' in so far as the praise covers all of my dog's antics. In my mind I am praising him for getting back on track and taking those last two jumps, but *MY DOG DOES NOT KNOW THIS.* There is no way my dog can recognize this. He cannot read my mind nor dissect his actions and separate the one I'm praising!**
>
> **All that my dog knows is that he can run amok and have a grand old time and that I am happy.**
>
> **Rather than stop the dog the moment he got off track and <u>SHOW</u> him how to succeed, I allowed him to self-amuse—and then praised him for it!**
>
> **This poor dog has no way of understanding what I liked and what I didn't. I have been very unclear. I have given blanket praise.**

If praise is given freely and unwarranted, without clarity or direction, it will not achieve the proper and desired result. Sure, your dog will be elated at being praised for no apparent reason other than just being in your presence, but this will do nothing towards teaching your dog the skills you want him to understand and perform for your particular sport.

Be fair to your dog: praise for specific behaviors and skills. Be particular to what you are praising, be exact. And then praise copiously!

Don't just get the job done: work constantly towards your perfect picture and praise for specific actions.

4.8.2 PRAISING INACCURACIES

This is perhaps the most common 'errant' praise. Praising inaccuracies is praise that is given for sloppy work, work that does not satisfy the picture you are training towards.

It is praise that is given simply because the dog eventually stumbles through and somehow manages to do what is being asked. But in no way does this practice further the journey towards that 'Perfect Picture'.

Consider a basic 'come' or 'here' command, a command all performance dogs are taught. When given, this command means stop what you're doing and come directly to me—at least in my own vision of a perfect recall.

But let's say I call my dog and he actually does acknowledge my command by stopping and looking back at me, but decides he wants to first check out a smell over to one side, which he does. I call again. He hesitates, sniffs some more, then reluctantly and without too much interest (his focus is still on whatever he is smelling) finally makes his way over to me.

I praise him copiously, am thrilled that he finally condescended to come to me.

This is ERRANT PRAISE, for sure.

I have praised him for a job that was half-hearted and sloppy solely because he finally, ultimately, grudgingly deigned to acknowledge my presence.

In my heart of hearts I'm hoping that my praise is going to somehow make him want to come to me more directly in the future, and with more desire. This, ladies and gentlemen, is called wishful thinking.

Instead of stopping the unwanted behavior and showing him what it is that I truly want in my 'perfect' recall picture, I praise him for stumbling through in the hopes that in future he will 'get it'.

To use the vernacular, "It ain't gonna happen."

Don't confuse your dog. Be clear in your training and praise!

First of all, my dog cannot read my mind, so he has no idea what I'm thinking he should do. Therefore there is no way in the future that he can possibly decide to perform the recall the way I want it to be performed IN MY MIND. **That picture is in MY MIND, NOT HIS!**

My dog only knows that I am praising what he is doing. Quite frankly, he's happy as he is not only getting to do what he wants to do, but I'm thrilled with his choice!

Worse, I have basically informed my dog that when I call him he is permitted to take a scenic route. There is no rush, thank you very much. Take your time. You can come when you're ready. Ha!

Then someday during a performance I am going to call him towards me to take an obstacle or to come to front or the like and he is going to stop and sniff and take his time and I am going to be most unhappy.

Yet this behavior is something I fostered, an activity I encouraged in training, something I did not check in training—even praised!

In my dog's mind there is no difference in what he has done in the ring and what he has done many times in training, yet suddenly I am unhappy. *Now he's confused.*

In my estimation, this is utterly unfair.

Wishful thinking is a totally unjust approach to training. It is my responsibility as his trainer to **SHOW HIM** what it is I want and **HOW TO SUCCEED.**

> *Remember:*
> *What you have in training is what you take into your performance!*

So if your dog is not executing a skill or behavior to your satisfaction, let him know immediately. Then show him how to succeed. Stop any confusion before it surfaces. You both will be happier in the end…

4.8.3 MISPLACED PRAISE

Misplaced praise is praise that is given when the handler does the work rather than the dog.

Misplaced praise is the handler praising the dog for a job well done when in actuality the dog does not do the skill or behavior on his own: the handler intervenes and does the work for the dog, hoping the dog will catch on.

It's imperative to realize that from the dog's point of view he need never become responsible or accountable: he simply needs to be in the area.

> *Example:*
>
> I signal my dog to take a particular jump, a skill he knows really well, has done a zillion times. My dog heads that way, appears committed, but suddenly veers off and fails to take the jump.
>
> I tell him 'Nice try', then call him over and tap the jump. He looks at it. I tap it again and he moves towards it.
>
> I praise him like he just conquered Mount Everest.
>
> **We continue on...**

In this example, the dog has learned nothing except that he really doesn't have to be responsible. Whatever he does, I'm not only going to do the work for him, I will be delighted with him for giving me that chance!

Misplaced praise does not show the dog how to do the skill right **the first time.** Worse, by praising the dog for work that you, the handler, have done, you are teaching the dog that the skill/behavior is a two-stage event: the dog sort of does what the skill calls for, then you finish it off so that it looks the way you want it to. This is two steps, not one.

For the dog this two-stage approach becomes the way the behavior is meant to be performed!

Because the dog has never had the opportunity to perform it correctly himself and by himself, this interference by the handler actually becomes part of the behavior.

> ### *Another Example:*
>
> Your dog lags while practicing a Rally or Agility Course, Heeling in Obedience, etc. You call, you encourage, you slap your thigh and plead with him to please play the game your way, but to no avail. Once the exercise is finished, you praise him with gusto.
>
> Realize that in your dog's mind, he thinks he just did a wonderful job. You just told him he did! Why try harder? Why change?
>
> ### *This is 'Misplaced Praise.'*

Rather than praising the dog for work that you, yourself, are doing, show the dog how to do it right by himself, without your assistance—and then let him do so! In other words, *show him how to succeed* and then have him repeat the skill or exercise so that he can succeed without your interference.

Let's look at the earlier example of the failure of the dog to jump: Stopping the dog the moment he bypasses the jump indicates to him that he has made a mistake. Taking him back and insisting that he take the jump would show him how to do it properly. The next step would be to allow him to perform the skill on his own, to succeed on his own. Repeat the entire sequence without interfering. Once he has done the jump cleanly and on his own, absolutely praise—and be sure the praise is enthusiastic and sincere.

Likewise in training if my dog is lagging while I'm heeling or running a course, I would stop immediately and let him know that his behavior is unacceptable (a check on the collar or putting on a short leash so that he cannot lag, whatever the situation calls for). Next I would repeat the behavior and allow him to succeed on his own. Then and only then would I go ballistic with praise!

> ### *Example:*
>
> Let's say I've just called my dog to me and he's slowly making his way towards me. It's obvious his heart is not in it. His head is swiveling left and right and though he's coming, he's creeping towards me as if it's a real effort.
>
> I am NOT happy with this attitude, so I slap my thigh and tell him to 'Hurry'. His pace does not change one little bit. I slap my leg some more and use a more encouraging voice until he finally reaches me—and even though he never once changed pace, I praise copiously.
>
> This is a prime example of 'misplaced praise.' I did all the work and cheerleading, my dog never responded—or understood that a response was required. My behavior was part of his picture!

What I should have done in the above example is first of all, be sure my dog understands what the 'hurry' command means. Once I am confident he knows the hurry command and yet still fails to respond when I give it, I can calmly walk towards him, take his collar, give it a check as I run backwards and repeat, *"Hurry! Yes, that's hurry."* I am showing him what I want. I am also making him responsible.

Then I can set him up for another recall so that he has the opportunity to succeed **on his own.** Once he comes barreling in and reaches me, I will praise with gusto, reward and interact. *It's party time!*

4.9 CHAPTER REVIEW

- ✓ The praise you give your dog is an outward expression of your approval and must always be the ***primary*** reward you give your dog.

- ✓ Avoid bribing your dog when training. Avoid bribing your dog into performing. Avoid bribing your dog into being your team partner. In the end it won't work. Teamwork will be impossible, as the dog will not be working for you or with you: the dog will only be working for the bribe.

- ✓ Having a dog that truly enjoys being <u>with</u> you, wants to be with you, and is eager to do things with you is in my estimation the real essence of teamwork—and a major reason why I enjoy training and performing with my dogs.

- ✓ My sincere praise (attitude), my ability to let my dogs know that I am delighted with their progress and their attitude, results in a faster learning curve and a higher success rate.

- ✓ Utilizing the *Four-Stage Release Program* insures that I am constant in my praise, that I am highlighting specific behaviors and skills (attention required!), and that I am developing teamwork based on understanding and appreciation and enjoyment.

- ✓ **Praise often. Praise with sincerity. Praise with honest joy. You can never praise too much...**

CHAPTER 5: PLAY and INTERACTION!

What to expect in this chapter:

- Building the 'Want to'
- What is 'interactive'?
- Defining self-amusement
- The importance of play
- The 3-5 approach
- Attention games
- How to play
- Getting a quick release
- Chapter Review

5.1 INSPIRING THE "WANT TO"

During the teaching phase, your dog is taught the 'how to': he is taught 'how to' execute the desired skill/behavior you are instructing him in. But teaching the 'how to' does not necessary instill his 'want to'. He can be shown how to accomplish something, yet have absolutely no desire or drive to perform it.

> ### The "WANT TO" is established during the teaching stage!

The 'want to' is rarely an attitude you can simply plug in later after all desire or drive has been obliterated through lack of use. Inspiring your dog to 'want to' be your team partner must be a major part of your dog's learning phase.

Certainly using the Four Stage Release Program (see Chapter 4) will play a major role towards exciting your dog's attitude and instilling 'want to' and self-confidence. **Praise will be primary.** The added reinforcement of play, however, will significantly strengthen and deepen your dog's 'want to' attitude.

To maintain the 'want to', you need to motivate, to inspire your dog—and play is an exciting and invigorating way to do so.

INTERACTIVE PLAY IS A GREAT MOTIVATOR!

5.2 PRESSURE VALVE RELEASE SYSTEM

When teaching, fine tuning, or drilling a dog on some technique or skill, it's a given that we will be putting certain demands on our dogs to perform. Some degree of mental exertion is inherent to the nature of any learning situation.

In grade schools children are given a recess to expend some energy and regroup for more classroom teaching. Recess wakes them up, refreshes them and allows them to be more open to further instruction.

For our dogs, we can use play to relieve any pressures. Play is a wonderful way to get rid of that pent-up energy and alleviate any psychological duress, freeing them to continue their training while still very much enjoying the process.

Besides making training enjoyable and building a stronger working relationship, introducing play into your training regimen gives your dog a physical outlet for his natural energies.

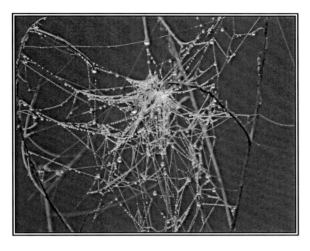

Play also helps to get rid of the mental cobwebs, to clear the mind so that it can better assimilate the information it is receiving.

Play is a beneficial release in that it stimulates, revitalizes, energizes—and above all, enormously enhances the relationship between you and your dog. Play brings you even more closely together as partners and a team.

> **Play is a motivational break for both the mind and the body.**

5.3 WHAT IS 'INTERACTIVE'?

Interactive play is play that requires that there be a physical and spiritual connection between you and your dog when you engage in play while training.

During interactive play you and your dog are relating, building a bond and higher regard for one another. A sound relationship and deeper understanding develops through interactive play. Interactive play results in mutual respect.

Additionally, interactive play means that your dog is continually coming <u>into</u> you for that play: the play is not something done without you. You are the main hub of his enjoyment. The toy is merely a tool connecting you both.

When you play with your dog during your training sessions, the interaction must occupy your focus. The play will require your full attention in order for it to be interactive. You and your dog are playing in concert; you're connected.

Tossing a toy or tennis ball repeatedly while your dog runs out, retrieves it, drops it at your feet for you to again pitch out for him cannot accurately be called interactive play. This is more akin to exercise. It's great, don't get me wrong. And it has its place. But it is not intimate, it is not truly interactive. Nor is it easy to do when training.

In fact generally it is the dog that controls a simple ball-pitching/retrieving situation. When we engage in this retrieving exercise, we basically become a human catapult, a human "Chuck It"® toy.

For many dogs it hardly matters who is tossing the ball—and that's what makes this more of a workout versus being truly interactive with a one-on-one exchange. There is little to no mutual interrelationship, no exchange or mental communion between dog and human.

However, if I toss a toy and when my dog brings it back, I engage in a game of tugs or play hide and seek with the toy, then I am guiding the dog's focus back onto me and we are now connected. We have contact and are strengthening a bond and understanding.

Lynn and Magnum engage in interactive play.

The toy is merely an implement I am using to connect with my dog—sort of like using a spoon to eat my soup: the spoon is an implement, but it's the soup that is of real importance. Likewise, the toy is simply a utensil to help me engage and bond with my dog.

By bringing the dog's focus onto me and making that connection between us more important than the toy retrieve itself, I have made the play interactive. The toy has less merit and pleasure than being in my company, which becomes my dog's primary desire.

Staying by me and interacting, receiving my attentions and camaraderie is his primary reward, not the act of retrieving the ball.

Again, let me say that ball retrieving is great fun and definitely has its place. I toss toys & balls for my dogs all the time, and they especially love it when I toss balls into the bay.

Physical exercise is a must for our beloved dogs. Hands down. When you are working with your dog, trying to teach him a performance skill, absolutely introduce randomized play throughout the training session—but keep it interactive.

Interactive means that you are a part of that play. There is communion between you and your dog. You are building a bond.

> ## TEST YOUR INTERACTIVE PLAY:
>
> **Toss a toy out for your dog a few times.**
>
> 1. Does your dog bring it back each and every time? If yes, great. If no, then you need to make it understood that your dog bring it directly back to you. Remember: that toy is yours. Your dog must respect that. You are not there to fetch and carry for him☺.
>
> 2. Does your dog come back directly, or does he take a scenic route to smell something or check something out? Do not allow this. Let him know he needs to come back directly. He is not allowed to ignore you! YOU are in charge.
>
> 3. When your dog returns the toy, do you immediately take it and pitch it out for him again? This is fun, to be sure: but it is not as interactive as it should and can be.
>
> 4. Do you engage in one-on-one play when the toy is returned? If not, you should. The one-on-one play is interactive with a direct link between you and your dog. Furthermore it fosters your dog's desire to **WANT** to be with you more.

5.4 WHAT IS SELF-AMUSEMENT?

Your dog is amusing himself if, when you toss a toy out for him, he grabs the toy and runs away with it. The toy is the target and the dog's primary concern, not you.

Your dog is amusing himself if he grabs a toy (tossed or not) and does victory laps or takes the toy away and begins to toss it up into the air himself, catch it, toss it again, maybe gnaw on it a bit. The dog is oblivious to your presence. Handler not required, thank you very much.

Your dog is amusing himself when he suddenly simply walks off during training to go and investigate a leaf that just fluttered down, or another dog that came into view, or to sniff something that grabbed his attention as he went by.

This is a dog that feels he has many options, is not focused on the handler, is not all that concerned about the handler, and furthermore, can have a lot a fun without the handler.

These are distractions your dog **learns**. Make no mistake. They are **learned** behaviors, and they are learned because the dog has lots of down time during the training session, is bored, and is left to his own devices.

Dogs are intelligent. They need mental stimulus as much as physical stimulus. When left on their own, they will find ways to entertain themselves.

5.5 SELF-AMUSEMENT NOT!

When working with your dog you should try hard to always be engaged with him in some way. In other words, you need to be paying attention to him. Do not give your dog the opportunity to learn unwanted behaviors!
Be with him. Pay **attention**.

If circumstances make this too difficult or even impossible (someone has approached you and wants to talk or you need to set up some equipment or the like), then you should put your dog up. Cease training and crate your dog—or at the very least, put your dog in a "Settle" at your feet and keep him near you so that he is not left to his own devices and inadvertently learn undesirable behaviors.

If you ignore your dog—give him the opportunity to entertain himself while you are otherwise engaged—then your dog is going to learn to ignore you. This is a behavior you do NOT want to encourage! And as the trainer, it is all up to you.

This dog is amusing herself, looking for something to play with: human not required.

It is counterproductive to allow your dog to self-amuse himself.
If your dog is stimulating and entertaining himself, why does he need you?

Imagine this picture: you are at the beach playing in the surf having a great time when suddenly your best friend interrupts you and begins pulling you to the car while telling you that you have to stop now, as it's time to go to the library and study. Hello? Really?

It is the same for your dog: if he is self-amusing and having fun without you and you suddenly jar him away from that fun and demand that he now go to work, he is not going to be a willing, enthusiastic partner.

Not the best of all possible situations, to be sure.

You are suddenly paying some attention to your dog, demanding teamwork, but have failed to establish that team spirit. It doesn't work that way.

Dogs are not tools or creatures born to do your bidding: they are individuals, have their own unique personalities, and must be nurtured properly in order for them to truly be a team partner.

The healthiest way to avoid allowing your dog to ignore you is to never allow it to happen to begin with. When you are in the company of your dog—and especially when you are teaching or training—be **WITH** your dog. *And I mean **WITH** him.*

This means your **attention** is completely on your dog. You are working directly with him at all times, you are aware of his movements, your focus is concentrated entirely on what your dog is doing and how he is doing it. You are alert to his body language, his ear set, tail set, and his overall **attitude**. The moment he exhibits any hesitations or signs of confusion, you are there for him!

Remember the need for attention and attitude... YOUR ATTENTION AND ATTITUDE!

Again: during any intermissions or interruptions, you should either crate your dog or have him lie down and be quiet until you are able to resume your interactive training.

Certainly another option (if feasible!) is to pick him up.

Rather than having to deal with a dog that has developed the habit of amusing himself and no longer requires your assistance, never allow the unwanted behavior to ever start. Simple.

NEVER ALLOW YOUR DOG TO IGNORE YOU!

5.6 SUSTAINING ATTENTION

Attention is a two-way street: in order to keep your dog's attention, you need to give him attention in return. To demand that your dog's attention never waver while you have a friendly chat with an acquaintance is entirely unfair.

More importantly, the more attention you give your dog, the more your dog is going to WANT to give you his undivided attention in return.

> *Attention is a two-way street:*
> *it goes both ways!*

So when you are with your dog, be <u>with</u> him—and by that I mean you are focused on him. You are aware of his every move. You are aware of his every mood. You are alert to his needs, his weaknesses, his strengths. He needs to be more than your canine buddy: he needs to be your teammate.

Maintain the "want to"! Motivate!!!

> *Stay focused. Avoid distractions.*

Staying constantly focused on your dog when training is not easy. However, it can and should be your primary consideration.

*When not engaged,
put your dog in a settle
until you return.
Don't allow
unwanted behaviors
to develop.*

Ways to start zeroing in on your dog & avoid distractions:

1. Talk to your dog. A lot. *And mean it*☺. (Remember the Canine Trinity™ your dog will recognize your sincerity!)

2. If you need to get a piece of equipment or replenish your treat supply, either take your dog with you or put the dog in a settle or in a crate while you do what is necessary. Do not allow him to wander; do not ignore him.

3. Should you find you are unable to concentrate because you are worried about some other extraneous matter that is constantly interrupting your thoughts, quit training for the day. Take your dog for a stroll instead; work out your private concerns while you walk.

4. When someone approaches you to ask about your beautiful dog or to say hello, how's it going, and so forth, break off your training, relax your dog or engage him in some interactive tugs while you respond to the interruption. Do not allow your dog to wander; do not ignore him.

5. Better still, if someone interrupts your training, simply and quickly explain that you are training and will be delighted to talk with them later.

6. Maintaining focused attention is no easy trick. Begin small and slowly develop your ability to sustain it. Start by concentrating your focus in short spurts and gradually increase that time frame.

All of us want 100% attention from our dogs when we're working with them; it's only fair to give 100% attention back to them. This absolutely makes for better teamwork!

> *Remember: You need to give as much as you want in return.*

So when you are with your dog, keep focused on your dog! Don't lose track, get side-tracked, be thinking about other things. Either be there with and for your dog, or quit for the day.

If you are not able to concentrate on your dog and the task you are working on, you will simply be spinning your wheels and going in circles. Certainly you will not be able to improve on anything, teach anything, or in anyway go forward with your training.

> **NEVER ALLOW YOUR DOG TO IGNORE YOU.**
> **Likewise, don't ignore your dog!**

5.7 THE IMPORTANCE OF PLAY

Play should be regularly and consistently integrated into your training program. Your dog should not make distinctions between playing and working—and it's up to you to make sure your dog believes that there is no difference between work and play.

> *Training and Play = ONE!*

Play should always be a constant in your training program and should NEVER be eliminated when teaching, training, or competing.

5.8 THE 3 TO 5 APPROACH:

It's very easy to become engrossed in something and keep going without realizing that we're overdoing. This is especially true if the activity is something the trainer is having difficulty with and so repeats and repeats and repeats in an effort to 'get it', not realizing that in the process the dog is fading and fading fast.

In order to prevent yourself from overdoing or from neglecting to interject play into your training program, I recommend the 3 to 5 approach. It's simple and goes like this:

After you do a skill, behavior, or exercise 3, 4, or 5 times *in a row*, have a bit of fun: play before continuing on.

- **Interject play.**
- **Engage with your dog.**
- **Interact.**

<u>Never</u> repeat a skill more than 5 times without interjecting play.

EXAMPLE:

I'm teaching my dog to understand his rear movement, so am having him do a number of rear leg cross-stepping skills (dog has front feet on a raised object and pivots around the object, driving with the rear legs by cross-stepping, also known as 'tucks'). I can do this 3-5 times, then whip out a toy and play. Repeat as needed☺.

The beauty of this approach is that you may repeat the same skill, behavior or exercise yet another 3 – 5 times, then play, and not be concerned about your dog's attitude. It will be upbeat.

Myst pivots on her disc

Play helps instill the 'want to'. Play is vital.

By constantly interrupting the training with some play, you are building the dog's desire to work. You are building the dog's drive. You are building the dog's attention. You are establishing a better relationship and bond with your dog: you are creating a team.

By habitually infusing play into your training regimen, your dog will never learn to make distinctions between work and play. For your dog, the two will be one.

Play is critical for establishing a bond between the dog and human.

5.9 ATTENTION GAMES

Attention games are interactive games you can play with your dog to help keep the dog focused and energized and ready to rock and roll.

Some games require the use of a toy, others do not. All attention games require interaction between dog and handler; they are not games that can be done solo. Handler is attentive to dog, dog is reciprocating in kind. It's a win/win situation.

Here are a few I routinely use:

1. The 'One, Two, Three' Game:

This is one of my favorites and I use it a lot. This game **ALWAYS** ends in play, but can be integrated into any training situation in order to establish and sustain drive.

Basically, it goes like this:

My dog will be in a sit or down or whatever is appropriate to the situation, and he will be told to stay or wait. I will count '1...2...3...', using an enticing, teasing tone. The dog MUST remain in place until I release him **after** giving the '3' count.

The release will be a command of some sort, such as 'Over' or 'Let's go!' or whatever word fits the particular skill or exercise I'm working on. Then, and only then, is my dog permitted to move.

Once the dog performs whatever it is we're working on, he is immediately released into me and engaged in play of some sort.

The teasing, tempting tone when you count '1, 2, 3' (with tantalizing pauses as you count) grabs the dogs attention and he quickly learns that something **fun** is about to happen.

Example...

Reba's attention is riveted on her handler as Ruth begins the '1,2,3' count. All of Reba's body language tells us she is ready for action.

The moment Ruth say's "Let's go!" after the '3' count, Reba is off with drive and enthusiasm!

As soon as Reba reaches Ruth, the two engage in interactive play.

Play is a wonderful motivator!

Should your dog break before the count of '3', immediately let him know that he can't do that, it's not part of the game. Do this with a quiet, "Uh-uh," or the like. He is then returned to the position from which he broke and *you will start the count all over again, right from the beginning.*

(Do not resume the count from where you left off when your dog broke. START THE COUNT ALL OVER, still using a teasing voice.)

When my Cattle Dog, Derby, would break after the count of '1' or '2', I would let her know that she had messed up, and man would she pitch a fit! She would bark at me and let me know in no uncertain terms that I was taking too long and to hurry up! This game truly jazzed her up—and she absolutely stayed focused on me.

CRATE GAME

When your dog is in a crate and you wish to get him out to perform, here is an easy and fun way to get him out with exuberance! *(Be sure he understands that he cannot just leap out, but must learn to wait for your release command.)*

1. **Open the crate door.**
2. **Count '1...2...3' in an enticing, promising way.**
3. **Give your release word and whip out a toy.**
4. **Dog flies out and into you with enthusiasm and excitement.**
5. **Play with him! Interact!**

Your dog is now ready to rock and roll.

With this game your dog learns to come out alert and energized and paying attention to you and you alone! Likewise, you are paying attention to him...

2. Twist, Spin, Unwind

This particular interaction does not ultimately require a toy or food, so can be used at performance venues without disrupting any other teams while still keeping your dog connected with you. Too, the activity helps to loosen the dog's spine and so is a healthy exercise as well.

It goes like this:

1. When <u>teaching</u> it, use a lure/treat (or clicker) to help your dog succeed.

2. Put the lure near the dog's nose and while keeping the head level, GUIDE his muzzle towards his rump.

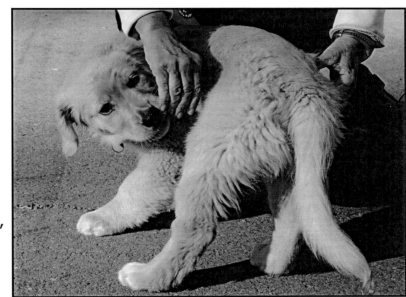

3. As your hand moves toward the dog's rear, give the activity a title, such as 'Twist', or 'Spin'.

4. Once the dog has done a full circle (it will look as though he's chasing his tail), reward him with the lure.

5. Repeat the above in the reverse direction.

You may wish to say 'Spin right' and 'Spin left', or 'Twist' for one direction and 'Spin' for the other, or 'Spin' and 'Unwind'. Be inventive. Have fun. It's a game, after all!

NOTE: Once your dog indicates that he understands the game, quickly remove the lure, generally after a week or so. Should you not remove the lure, your dog will fail to spin, twist or unwind without it. The lure will become a bribe—not something you want.

Naturally you may occasionally reward your dog, but be careful how you approach the reward. Give your dog a chance to succeed as your companion and partner: don't bribe.

3. Touch Game

This game is especially handy, as it not only brings the dog 'into you, it involves the dog lifting. As a consequence this game is more energizing.

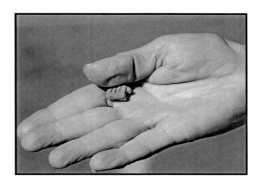

1. Again, begin with a lure in order to teach through success.

2. Hold the treat under your thumb in the palm of your hand while the remaining fingers remain extended out.

3. Lower the palm with the lure tucked under the thumb to your dog's nose.

4. Raise the palm upwards as you say 'Touch'.

5. As your dog lifts to get the cookie and touches your palm with his nose, release the cookie to him.

6. As he becomes proficient, have him 'Touch' 2-3 times in a row (saying 'Touch' each time) before releasing him to the cookie.

7. As ever, get rid of the lure/treat as quickly as possible.

(This can certainly also be taught using a clicker. You have the dog 'touch', then click, then treat.)

4. 'Pass Through' Game

The object of this game is that the dog 'pass' under one leg, come out and then 'pass' through the other. Again, this is a game to keep the dog active and connected with you, such that the dog is not being ignored and learning unwanted behaviors.

1. Stand with your legs somewhat apart.

2. Hold a cookie in each hand.

3. With your right hand, show the dog the lure, then guide him between your legs while giving a verbal command, such as 'Pass' or 'Through'.

4. Immediately take your left hand behind your left leg and switch it as a lure with the right hand. Your dog should now be focused on the treat in your left hand.

(After circling Esther's right leg, Jiminee is lured into another 'pass' through her legs and then is lured around her left leg, completing a Fig. 8 type of configuration.)

5. Using the left hand, draw the dog behind and around your left leg until the dog is now in front of you again.

6. You may release him here or take your right hand behind your right leg and switch the lure from your left hand to your right hand, then guide your dog back and around your right leg as well. This will result in your dog having done a figure 8 type movement between your legs.

5. Combinations of the Above!

Once your dog understands each of these games, you can begin to combine them.

> *Examples:*
> 1. **Combine a 'Spin' and 'Twist' with a 'Touch' afterwards.**
> 2. **Have your dog "Pass" and conclude with a "Touch".**
> 3. **Have your dog back up, then count '1,2,3' and have him fly into a 'Touch'.**
>
> *Be inventive!*

Play Builds Attitude And Eagerness, Which In Turn Strengthens Attention.

Remember: you, the handler, control the play. Only quit on your terms. More importantly, do not permit your dog to ignore you.

Should your dog decide he doesn't want to play with you anymore, that there is something more important he needs to attend to (such as checking out a smell nearby or marking the area to let Bubba know he was there), nip it in the bud straight away. Do not allow your dog to ignore you. Immediately stop the unwanted behavior and redirect your dog back onto you!

5.10 TOY AT THE READY

I train wearing a vest. I have different styles, different weights. Many are vests I've purchased from sport stores, found in the hunting department. (I particularly like the hunting vest as it has a large back pocket that works for toy storage.) One lady I know uses a vest designed for photographers. Whatever style, the vest must have pockets. Lots of pockets...

The vest allows me to keep food, toys, leashes, lids—any light training equipment I want or might need—on my person and at the ready.

My back pocket is reserved for toys. When I want to reward my dog with some play, I can whip out the toy without dropping a beat in my training process.

Certainly I don't want to have to run back to my setup for the toy. The toy is ALWAYS on my person.

Timing...the timing for the reward is important.

Rewarding my dog at that point where he is doing precisely what I want him to do has more impact and is more productive than having a time lapse between that moment when my dog performs the skill correctly and when I finally get around to rewarding and reinforcing him with play.

Too, because I always have the toy on me, my dog is always alert to the *possibility* of play interaction: he never knows when I might whip out that toy. **That anticipation is a powerful tool!**

However, if the toy is at my setup or in my training bag or the like, my dog is going to know this. Certainly he is!

Some small part of his mental focus is going to be thinking about that toy over yonder at my set up. My dog will not be focused entirely on me and what I might do at any given moment. This is contrary to my goal.

I do not want him distracted: I want him focused on me.

Note the back bulge in Steven's vest: his toy is at the ready.

For me, the vest works. Some prefer to tuck a toy behind in their waistband; others use an apron affair. The point is, have a toy on your person and ready to whisk out to reward, motivate, and reinforce your dog's understanding and progress.

Timing is central to training. Having the dog come 'into' you is crucial. Have the toy on your person and at the ready so that when you need it, it's there. Better yet, the toy and you become synonymous for your dog.

5.11 HOW TO PLAY

Perhaps "How to play" sounds like a foolish subject, but it's really not.

All dogs have prey drive. It's part of their genetic makeup. They are, after all, descendents of the wolf.

Naturally some dogs have more than others—even within the same breed—but nevertheless, all dogs come equipped with prey drive.

Too often trainers try to initiate play by shoving some smelly old toy in the poor dog's face, then shaking it right there at his nose and asking the poor dog if he wants it or not.

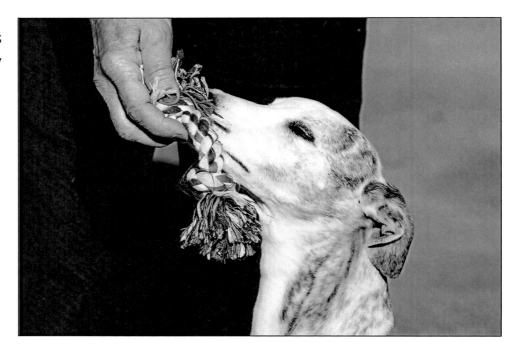

It's a rare (or desperate!) dog that will respond playfully to this assault.

Entice instead. Draw on a dog's natural prey drive.

Rather than stuff the toy into the dog's face, drag it away from him! Draw out his desire to chase a moving object. I can guarantee that you will get a more favorable response.

Additionally, when introducing play into your training, do not spend more time playing than training. If you do, the dog will most likely only want to play, not train. Play will carry more weight rather than being a valuable part of the training session.

Play is used to keep your *training alive!*™

It is also meant to alleviate some of the pressures mental concentration can induce—and make no mistake, any learning situation requires mental concentration. Introducing play into your training will release much of that pressure and afford you and your dog the ability to progress with greater ease and enjoyment.

Be sure to mix play into the training itself. Do NOT wait until your training session is over and then play. Should you do this, your dog will begin to get anxious during the training and ONLY look forward to the play at the end. Your training will be hindered. Worse, your dog will not learn to enjoy the skills you are teaching: those skills will only be something to get through in order to play.

So absolutely intersperse play throughout your training regimen.
Keep your ***Training Alive!*** ™

Remember: Play and training are one!

5.12 GETTING A QUICK RELEASE

Some dogs are not eager to surrender their toy once they retrieve it. I, personally, do not offer a food treat to teach the dog to give up his toy when I am playing with him. I find this approach counterproductive.

My purpose when playing is the play itself, the interaction, and I do not want my dog responding to food rather than to that interaction with me. Therefore I do not use a treat when I am playing with a toy.

Initially I will help the dog understand the concept of releasing the toy on command by holding the ends of the toy that are hanging out on either side of the dog's mouth and slipping my index fingers inside the dog's mouth and behind the toy. I then ease the toy out as I give a verbal command such as "Give" or "Out" or "Release." The verbal command is essential so that the dog understands the association between my command and the release.

Once the toy is released, I praise. I will initially use A LOT of verbal praise when my dog releases a toy on command, but I will not use a treat. Again, I want my dog engaged with me, not simply responding so that he can get a treat. Playing with me IS the treat☺.

As I said before, some dogs have higher prey drive than others. With dogs that have really high prey drive, the above approach may not be sufficient. So with dogs that have high prey drive, I use this approach: again take hold of both sides of the toy (not one side, but BOTH sides) and hold the toy against

your body such that the dog can no longer rip and tear or play tugs with the toy. The toy is held stationary and so becomes less attractive to the dog. Give your verbal release command and keep the toy held against you.

The dog will eventually release it. ***Praise, praise, praise.***

Be sure that once the toy is back in your hand that the dog does not lunge for it or in any way try to take control of the toy again. Remember: that toy is yours! Your dog must respect this.

If you have a dog that feels the toy is his and tries to rip it out of your hands unbidden, teach him to "Leave it." (See chapter one.) He must learn to not take the toy without your permission, just as he must not dive into his dinner without your consent.

You are the pack leader. Do not allow your dog to control these situations.

Teaching a Toy 'Leave it'

1. **Hold your dog's collar in order to control his movement.**

2. **Hold out the toy and tell your dog to 'Leave it.'**

3. **If your dog lunges, give the collar a check by popping it as you again tell him to 'Leave it.'**

4. **Once you feel your dog cease resisting and accept your ownership of the toy (you will feel him relax via your hold on the collar), take your hand off the collar while still holding the toy out. Do not hide the toy when you do this. That would defeat the purpose. Keep the toy visible and inviting.**

5. **If your dog ignores your 'leave it' command and lunges at the toy once the collar pressure is released, immediately take his collar and give him a more vigorous check. Let him know in no uncertain terms that his behavior is unacceptable. That toy is yours and he must respect that.**

6. **As your dog accepts your ownership, you can deepen his understanding by shaking the toy or giving it a light toss as you tell him to 'leave it.'**

7. **If your dog accepts your leadership position, then by all means pick up the toy and reward him with some play! (But remember: you pick up the toy. Do not send your dog for it. All good things come from you!)**

5.13 CHAPTER REVIEW

In order for your dog to 'want to' be your team partner and perform whatever venue you have chosen with enthusiasm and spirit, you need to make the training positive and upbeat. Praise will of course be your primary reward. Nothing can surpass praise—and praise is something you can take everywhere with you.

But interjecting play into your daily training routine will greatly enhance the relationship you are building with your canine buddy as well as making the learning process easier and enjoyable for all concerned.

The play must, however, be interactive. You need to be attentive to your dog while engaged in play and the dog must be partnered with you in order for play to occur.

The dog cannot simply choose a toy and run off to amuse himself. The play should be a joint effort binding you and your dog in a single activity and so unifying you.

Introducing the "3-5 approach" (page 114) will help make play a natural part of your training routine. Play and training will be one. There will be no difference. As a consequence, you and your dog will not only find training enjoyable, you'll find that your training will progress more rapidly and with more focus.

More enjoyment means greater attitude; greater focus means greater attention. With greater **attitude** and greater **attention,** you have a stronger relationship: you have **teamwork.**

Remember: Play and training are one!

Chapter 6: Train, Train, Train

What to expect in this chapter:

- ◆ Routine required
- ◆ No bored dogs
- ◆ *Training Alive!*™
- ◆ To drill or not to drill
- ◆ What to do during 'downtimes'
- ◆ Doodling
- ◆ Quality vs. quantity
- ◆ Run-throughs
- ◆ Chapter review

What you have in training is what you take into the ring.

6.1 ROUTINE REQUIRED

Your training should have stability and regularity. Stability and regularity are enormous benefits in helping your dog learn and understand and ultimately have the confidence he needs so that he can be a more flexible, reliable team partner all around.

It would be a rare football coach who would tell the team players, "Just come and train when you can. No big deal."

And that is because training with consistency IS a big deal. If any football team doesn't train routinely on a fixed schedule, the players will never achieve true teamwork, let alone stand a chance of succeeding on game day.

What this means is that you should establish a training schedule that is moderately constant and steady.

I personally schedule my training time into my daily timetable. This way I am assured of getting my training in. I am not leaving it to chance, nor putting it off.

It is all too easy to procrastinate, especially after a hard day at work. By scheduling in my training time I stand more of a chance of actually getting it done. As a bonus, I often find that the training sessions revive me, as they usually end up being an invigorating and mentally uplifting workout rather than a drag. It's an outcome that works for both me and my dog☺.

Being with my dog and playing with my dog while we train revitalizes me. And the more regular I am with my training schedule, the more I look forward to it—as does my dog. Training then becomes a significant part of the day, one I anticipate with relish.

6.2 PRACTICE WITH ATTENTION

I cannot state often enough how critical it is that during your practice sessions you do not ignore your dog nor allow your dog to ignore you.

To ignore your dog or allow your dog to ignore you is a blueprint for unhappiness—**IF** you are hoping to have teamwork and be able to perform to the level you aspire to.

Teamwork requires mutual attention. The dog must pay attention to you and your commands; likewise, you must pay attention to your dog so that you can better

> *Attention is a two-way street: do not ignore your dog, and your dog will not learn to ignore you.*

understand him and subsequently teach and direct him towards the goal you are working towards with greater ease and less confusion.

Stopping to praise a specific response, interjecting periods of play, recognizing your dog's attitude (confidence, enjoyment or confusion, fear), and having control of your practice sessions will not only improve your dog's attention, but will also enhance your ability to zero in and see more, be more, and do more.

6.3 MY DOG IS BORED—NOT!

When my dog is with me, how could he possibly be bored? I am the apple of his eye, am I not? If I am the center of my dog's world and he is in my company, he cannot possibly be bored.

To say that my dog is bored when working with me might just be a reflection of myself as a handler, trainer, companion, or team leader. I need to look carefully into this mirror and be objective.
Some questions I need to ask are:

1. Is my dog truly bored—or is that confusion? Have I been fair and clear when training? Does he really understand what is required? Or is he shutting down?

2. Is my dog's lack of enthusiasm the result of my not interjecting enough play into our training sessions? Has our training become grueling and repetitive rather than motivating and alive?

3. Do I ignore my dog more than I realize when we train? Is there more downtime than companionship and teamwork when we train?

4. Does my dog demonstrate a lack of purpose? Meaning I don't praise enough and give his responses incentive or direction?

Be honest with yourself. Quite frankly I often see a handler absolutely convinced that the dog 'knows' how to execute some skill, when in actuality the dog's understanding of what is being asked is vague, way too general, and without true clarity. This dog is lost in a 'Gray Zone' and cannot possibly succeed to expectations.

Be honest and be fair.

If you think your dog is 'bored', look towards yourself, not the skill, not the exercise, not the performance. Your dog is a best friend. Treat him as such.

Be honest and be fair.

If during training you are attentive to your dog, it's highly unlikely that your dog could ever become bored.

Boredom occurs when there is a lack of stimulus. YOU need to be the stimulus behind your teamwork. Maintain **attention** and train with an upbeat **attitude** and your dog will never be bored!

Be honest and be fair.

In part being fair means not demanding more than your dog can give. If you are demanding more than is possible, your dog may shut down. This is not boredom, this is self-preservation.

> **If you feel that your dog is bored with a skill you are working on, reassess your approach. Ask yourself the following:**
>
> 1. Does my dog understand what I am asking?
> 2. Does my dog know how to succeed in the specific skill we are working on?
> 3. Am I praising appropriately?
> 4. Am I interjecting <u>interactive</u> play into our training?

Every leader needs to understand the limitations and strengths of each member of the team in order to best utilize each member's strong points and avoid pushing anyone beyond his abilities.

Knowing your dog's limitations and strengths is a very important part of your job as team leader.

Not all humans can leap tall buildings in a single bound. Some humans are aggressive, some shy, some are strong, others are weak, some are charming, others are dour: character varies. Every human is an individual with his own strengths and foibles. This is true of dogs as well.

Every dog is unique...

Certainly you do not want to demand more from your dog than he is able to give. This would be utterly unfair, maybe even impossible. This could develop into a situation where all parties concerned are frustrated, unhappy, even defeated. Be fair.

By the same token, you most certainly do want to emphasize and expand those attributes that your dog excels in and can succeed in.

Learn to read your dog, see where his talents lie☺.

Step back and really observe your dog. Attempt to understand his individuality.

During your training sessions look carefully at your dog. Work at understanding him. **Remember:** he is unique. He has his own personality.

Pay attention to your dog and his reactions to various stimuli and demands. Be objective and honest, then adjust your training to accommodate and optimize your approach based on what you have learned.

In other words, accept the pros and cons and adapt: do what is necessary to make you and your dog a team!

But if you believe your dog is bored, look to yourself: you are the one making the demands, instructing and conducting the training situation. Figure out what changes you need to make in order to make your ***Training Alive!*** ™

6.4 TRAINING ALIVE!™

Keeping your *Training Alive!* ™ should be enjoyable as well as gratifying. After all, that's why we work with our dogs: they're our companions and teammates! The time training, however, needs to be alive, not flat—and only you, the team leader, can decide how it's going to go.

When training you must have focus, be concentrated on the small steps in your dog's progress, and be alert to any signs of confusion in your dog or deviations from your ultimate purpose. In other words, don't allow yourself to get sidetracked.

One of my 'Golden Rules' is that it's your everyday training that you take into competition. It's not possible to go into a competition and suddenly have an alert, eager and dynamic canine teammate if that energy and enthusiasm is not also expressed in your training.

In order to avoid having your training sessions disintegrate and be non-productive, one of the things you can do is to train with your final goal in mind at all times. Have a mental picture of what you want each particular exercise or skill to look like, and when training, accept nothing less than progress towards that image, that goal.

It's very easy is to fall into a rut and not be aware that your training has become ho-hum and that you have deviated from your goal. It's necessary that you learn to be objective and LOOK. Watch what your dog is doing at all times, and ask yourself if that behavior is what you want in the end product?

If it is, be jubilant. Express your pleasure. Let your dog know that you are thrilled with his performance.

If not, it is your job as the trainer to first of all stop the unwanted behavior **as it is happening**. Do not allow the behavior to proceed. Then take your dog back to the point where the undesired behavior began and **show** your dog how to succeed. That you show your dog how to succeed is critical. Do **not** expect your dog to guess how you want the skill performed: show him!

Once you have shown him how to properly perform that particular skill, let him repeat it and succeed on his own merit without your assistance. Once accomplished, be overjoyed! Express your delight. Don't be shy☺.

It's easiest to stop an unwanted behavior by recognizing the beginnings of it and taking the proper steps to deter it immediately, as stated above. This also contributes to your having a confident dog, one who understands and so is enjoying the training.

So one of the first things you need to begin incorporating into your training is the ability to recognize the beginnings of any problem, and in order to do that you have to have a mental picture of what your final goal is. This is essential. Without that visual endpoint in view, you will have nothing to compare your development against, and it is then that your training can become stagnant. Don't get into a training rut. Keep a mental picture of what you want—and work towards that target in every training session.

Honest **PRAISE** is another essential ingredient to keeping your *Training Alive!*™

When your dog does something you truly like, let him know. Tell him!
And I don't mean simply shoving a cookie in his face:
I mean verbally and physically expressing your pleasure at your dog's accomplishment. You'll be amazed at the reception this approach will get!

Another vital element every training session should include is **PLAY**. Play releases pressure and allows both parties—trainer and dog alike—to take a mental break, interact, and maintain enthusiasm. In the best of all possible training sessions your dog should not be able to distinguish between what you are teaching and the play: the two should be so intertwined that they are impossible to tell apart. ***Learning and play are one.***

All dogs can learn to play. Some are more eager than others, certainly, but you can still teach the more introverted dog to play enough to interact and be more focused on you.

If you have a dog that is not responding to your play efforts, do not give up. Each time you train, train your dog to play as well. (see Chapter 5)

Remember: start with verbal encouragement and drawing out your dog's innate prey drive. Drag the toy ***AWAY*** from your dog. Do not wave it in his face! It is the movement of the toy that will draw out the prey drive in your dog. Eventually your dog will take one small step towards it. Praise him—and put the toy away.

Do not force the issue. Later repeat the process. Allow your dog to take 2-3 steps, then quit. Soon your dog is going to want that toy more and more.

Build his desire gradually. Do not push your dog into the play; allow the **dog** to build that drive!

Before you know it you will be actually be playing with your dog. What a joy!

Integrate the play into your training. This is important. Do NOT save the play for the end of the training session. **Remember:** you want your dog to consider his training and play to be one and the same.

What I recommend is that any skill or exercise be repeated 3-5 times, followed by some play. That same skill or exercise can then be worked on again, as long as play is thrown in every 3-5 repetitions. Using this approach prevents the repetition from ever being boring—especially if you are using honest praise as well.

So to keep your ***Training Alive!***™ always train with a mental picture of how you want it performed, employ honest praise, and interject play throughout the training session. Not only will you and your canine buddy find greater enjoyment training, you will discover that you are progressing more quickly than you ever imagined. It's a win/win approach.

6.5 TO DRILL OR NOT TO DRILL?

Repetition in training—what does that mean exactly? It means that a skill or exercise is repeated. Drilling a dog on a particular maneuver or skill ups the ante, so to speak: drilling a dog is repetition with an exponent. It's repetition repeated time and time again.

Is this bad? Absolutely not. In truth it is *only through repetition* that we or dogs or any sentient being learns. Repetition is mandatory in order to learn.

Learning involves establishing a neural network in the brain, then re-using this network time and time again. It's like building a bridge across a deep abyss: once the bridge is built, we have learned something new, and crossing the abyss becomes effortless. But if we fail to use the bridge regularly, we may become afraid to cross, or even forget that the bridge exists. It is the building process and regular use that makes the crossing effortless.

As a child I sang the 'Alphabet Song' time and time again, as do many children around the world—and to this day I can still sing it. This process was how I learned my ABC's. The alphabet was learned through repetition and the reason I repeated it over and over again as a child was because I was singing. The experience was enjoyable. The repetition didn't matter.

I can throw a ball for my dog time and time again and he never gets 'bored.' He may get tired, but not bored. Yet this is repetition. The reason he is not bored is that it is fun!

And that, ladies and gentlemen, is the crux of the matter: too many trainers look upon drilling in training as an onerous task, something one needs to get through but on no account enjoy, sort of like being stuck in commuter traffic.

Or there's the other side of the coin where the handler is so-o-o worried and stressed, the training sessions become more like boot camp, where rigor and formality dominate. Repetition becomes a monotonous drill—and is about as desirable as the one in a dentist's office.

What is needed is some diversion in training. Trainers need to lighten up while simultaneously instilling the drive and work ethic needed in any performance venue. This means that play is NOT just something done between exercises, but is actually an inherent part of the exercise itself.

Repetition in training should not be traumatic, ugly...or boring.
On the contrary: repetition should be exciting, motivating, and alive!

6.6 DOWNTIMES

Certainly if you are working around others or with club equipment, there are going to be periods when you will not be able to practice some of the skills until it is your turn. These 'downtimes,' these lag periods, can be used to your advantage— and should be!

During Downtimes:
❖ Practice small skills.
❖ Play with your dog.
❖ Be engaged with your dog.
❖ Keep your dog focused on you.
❖ Observe your dog's demeanor and attitude: learn about your dog.
❖ Randomize skill commands and incorporate some of the skills into your play.
❖ Make training and being with you an upper, not a drag.

Keep dog engaged!

Downtimes are periods when dogs have the greatest opportunity to learn unwanted behaviors, so it's really important that you not ignore your dog during these lag times.

So if you are unable to remain engaged in some way with your dog during a downtime, crate him. At the very least have him settle into a down at your feet so that he is unable to 'amuse' himself and so develop nasty habits.

6.7 DOODLING WITH S.O.S.:
Stationary Operating System

To doodle is to draw or scribble in an idle fashion. We've all done a bit of scribbling at one time or another on the sides of a note page while listening to a teacher or professor lecture. It helps keep us awake while toning our artistic abilities☺.

Obviously doodling with our dogs is not going to involve any drawing or scribbling. Nevertheless, the doodling I'm going to discuss will certainly tone a dog's abilities as well as assist in keeping a dog awake—and alert!—during down times.

A 'Stationary Operating System' (hereafter referred to as S.O.S.) is doodling in place. Ultimately it's a fast-paced response to randomized commands given and executed in heel position. S.O.S. is performed to strengthen and sharpen a dog's response and understanding of each specific command.

S.O.S. is done in a fixed location. Doodling is not something one does while moving about a ring or while performing an obedience exercise. Doodling is the nimble performance of a set of moves that allows the handler to keep his dog from mentally fading. For this reason alone doodling can be a useful tool to have as a backup on any number of occasions.

Doodling with your canine partner is beneficial in numerous other ways:
- The dog is active (versus idling & fading).
- Handler and dog are in communication.
- Handler and dog are working in unison.
- There is a clarification of specific maneuvers for your dog.
- Each particular 'doodling' maneuver is individually sharpened.
- The command response to each move becomes faster.
- Handler and dog ultimately have a Stationary Operating System to utilize during down times.

So what does doodling involve? Basically it's the performance of moves your dog already knows, such as 'sit,' 'down,' and 'stand.' Your dog should be near you. Doodling is done in close proximity. It's meant to tone, to sharpen, and to sustain communication between you and your dog.

A doodling session with just these three moves could go as follows: "Prince, stand. Down. Sit. Stand. Sit. Down. Stand. Sit. Good boy!"

But as with so many things, you begin slowly…

Initially it might be necessary to use hand signals as well as verbals to help Prince understand this new game. (One such hand signal might be pointing to the ground for the 'Down' command.) As Prince becomes more proficient, speed up the process—and discontinue using the hand signals.

Once your dog is proficient with these simpler skills, more doodling moves can be added to his repertoire. Be inventive!

Other doodling moves to include could be pivoting in place. You could also include a sidestep directly to your right with an "In" command. Likewise, you could sidestep directly to your left with an "Out" command.

Nancy and Ticker are set up for doodling. Ticker is alert and ready to respond. They are connected.

Here is a photo series that can help you teach your dog the command "out", meaning to get up and move to the left. What command word you prefer to use is naturally of your own choosing.

Teaching "OUT"

We begin with the dog sitting in heel position.

STEP ONE: Bring your right foot in front of your left and slip it in between your left foot and your dog.

STEP TWO: Now bring your left foot around and behind your right foot and slide it in between your right foot and your dog.

STEP THREE: Align your left foot with your right foot.

STEP FOUR: Have your dog sit in heel position with 'Ready' attention.

Other additions could include a single stride forward with an "Up-sit" followed by one step backwards with a "Back" command. Turns performed in place are also very active and will keep your dog focused.

All of these moves can be mixed and matched, following no pattern. Randomize. Do not be predictable, or else your dog will start anticipating and performing without you.

Remember: Always Think <u>Teamwork</u>!

Naturally you will need to teach each individual skill separately before ever trying to incorporate it into your doodling drill. It would be utterly unfair to ask you dog to perform a skill he has never been taught, let alone to do it quickly in conjunction with other moves. So absolutely: teach first.

The command word that you use when doodling should be the same one you used when teaching each respective move. (The command words I am suggesting are simply examples.) Use words that your dog understands and that you are comfortable with.

Picture this scenario: you've warmed your dog up and the gate steward has motioned for you to approach the ring. You and Prince are primed. You're ready. But wait...what's going on? Why am I being waved away? What's with the delay? I may be ready, but obviously no one else is.

Darn. There goes all that warm-up.

You can feel Prince beginning to wilt beside you. And now you notice that he's paying more attention to the cute little Sheltie going by than he is to you. This is the time to pull out your ace-in-the-hole.

Launch your <u>S</u>tationary <u>O</u>perating <u>S</u>ystem!   Doodle!

> "Prince, ready? Good boy-o. Stand. Down. Up-sit. Stand back. About turn. In. Out. Good boy!! Around. Back, back. Out. Stand. Pivot. Excellent!! Are you ready? Steady...okay, let's go!"

And so you enter the ring with an alert, attentive, focused dog who is not only ready to perform, but is anxious to do so!

Doodling can be utilized whenever you need a focused dog but have limited time and/or space.

I've often doodled with my dog while anticipating a run-off in obedience. It actually serves as a nice warm-up. After all, presumably my dog's trained. He simply needs to be alert and attentive to perform what he's been trained for. Doodling is an excellent warmer-upper!

Doodling quickly centers the dog's focus. By the same token, because you must quickly issue commands and make sure they are obeyed to your satisfaction, you will be focused on your dog—always a favorable arrangement.

When doodling you are communicating with your dog while working WITH him. This is sound leadership and teamwork.

Let me reiterate: do not pattern train the doodling moves. Repeat the moves randomly. This will gradually hone your dog's knowledge of each maneuver and sharpen his precision in their performance.

With a trained dog I especially like to do what I call 'rapid fire doodling.' This is doodling done at a much faster pace—but only with dogs that know each exercise well. Rapid fire doodling helps teach a dog to respond quickly. It's also great fun!

Doodling is a wonderful means of keeping your dog's attention on you and not allowing him to become listless and foggy. This Stationary Operating System can be a useful tactic in a variety of situations, no matter the venue. So don't idle. Doodle.

6.8 QUALITY VS. QUANTITY

Some people can allot 15 minutes to their daily training regimen, others do not have time constraints (lucky them!). But overall the amount of time given to training is not nearly as important as how that training proceeds. It's what you do with that time that is of greatest import!

In this manual we have so far discussed Leadership, the Canine Trinity™, the Perfect Picture, Praise, and Play. It is now time to bring all of these elements together into your training program and so have the best training possible on any given day.

Even if you are unable to allot much time to your training session, you need to make that training count. It should have substance, merit, and purpose.

So remember:

WHEN YOU TRAIN: you need to be the **team leader.** Your dog depends upon this! It is your job to show him how to succeed; it is your job to give him direction; it is your job to be his tower of strength. It is your job to bring the best out in your dog.

WHEN YOU TRAIN: you need to keep in mind your dog's strengths and weaknesses and adjust accordingly. Understand your dog's senses (the **Canine Trinity™**) and what you can or need to do in order to help him succeed. As the team leader and trainer, this is your job!

WHEN YOU TRAIN: you should **always** work towards your **Perfect Picture** so that you don't waste your precious training time going through the motions of training and neither solidifying your dog's understanding nor making any progress whatsoever. Making the Perfect Picture your goal each and every time you train will contribute enormously to establishing clarity, consistency, progress and stability.

WHEN YOU TRAIN: Praise! Your dog is working with you solely to please you: let your dog know how pleased you are with him. **YOU** must be your dog's **primary** reward. So praise! Watch your dog's eyes light up and his attitude become buoyant, his desire to please become even more intensive. Praise is essential.

WHEN YOU TRAIN: Play. Intersperse interactive play using the 3-5 approach. Play should be an integral part of your training regiment. Your dog should not be able to detect a difference between work and play: the two are one.

> *Quantity is simply a number:*
> *QUALITY is the essence within.*
> *QUALITY is SUBSTANCE!*

If you are able to satisfy and incorporate all of these dynamics into your training, you will undoubtedly move towards attaining your goal, but more importantly, you will strengthen the bond between you and your dog through a greater understanding and respect for one another.

You will have teamwork!

> *What you have in training is what you take into the ring.*

6.9 RUN-THROUGHS

Once you have taught your dog how to perform the required skills pertinent to your particular sport, then you need to practice run-throughs.

Run-throughs are rehearsals. They are dry runs meant to prepare you for your ultimate competition.

Run-throughs are necessary on many levels.

Run-through perks:

- ❖ Give you and your canine companion practice completing an entire performance in one go.
- ❖ Give you a feel for your momentum, your timing.
- ❖ Give you the practice necessary to prepare for real competitions.
- ❖ Give you an overall perspective of your strengths and weaknesses.
- ❖ Give you the opportunity to work out any glitches.
- ❖ Give you practice establishing harmony and unity between you and your dog.

- ❖ Help your dog learn confidence under the pressure of performance.
- ❖ Help your dog stabilize his ability to work and concentrate despite the physical and environmental distractions associated with performance venues.
- ❖ Give you experience performing so that you become a better leader/handler.

In my estimation, run-throughs are a boon with more benefits than I can possibly enumerate. Perhaps the most important consequence of run-throughs is that you and your dog can become a better team.

6.10 CHAPTER REVIEW

Obviously the substance of your training is going to be reflected in the quality of your performance: what you have in training is what you take into competition. Training is important!

A training routine is vital if you want to succeed. Establish a schedule that works for you, one that allots regular time slots for your training.

A regular schedule allows for more consistent training—and repetition. Repetition is a valuable teaching method. In order for your dog to truly learn, you must embrace repetition in your training regimen.

Clarity is another essential ingredient that must be incorporated in all training sessions. Clarity allows for learning. Clarity dispels confusion.

A confused dog cannot learn and will eventually shut down. But if you show your dog precisely what it is you want him to do and show him how to succeed, your dog will not become confused. Just the opposite: clarity in training will result in a dog that is not only willing, but one that will have confidence and be eager to work.

Certainly PRAISE is imperative. Praise gives your dog purpose. If you are fair in training and show your dog precisely how to succeed, your dog will gladly respond in kind given your approval, which is **praise**!

Your **attitude** when working with your dog as well as your **attention** to the detail and what it is you must do to help your dog succeed is what will ultimately give you the success you are working so diligently towards.

It will result in **TEAMWORK.**

Train Regularly, Praise and Play!

Chapter 7: Become the RING MASTER!

What to expect in this chapter:
- Partnership required
- Preparation: key ingredient
- Desensitize dog
- Finding your "Show Gauge"
- "Goldilocks" syndrome
- It's Showtime!
- The "Right Stuff"
- Warm-ups
- Entering to compete
- Jackpots
- Chapter Review

BECOMING A RING MASTER IS THE CULMINATION OF YOUR TRAINING: IT IS THE **GRANDE FINALE!**

Your dog is working to the level of your *Perfect Picture* and you're convinced of his stability and understanding. You want to start competing and earning those titles and points you have been training for. Now more than ever, keeping focused and maintaining a positive mental outlook will be of major concern.

When performing, everyone basically has the same goals:

- ✓ You want to qualify.
- ✓ You want to do the best you possibly can.
- ✓ You want to enjoy the process.

If you are comfortable and understand what it is you need to do, your dog will be comfortable and so be able to do his job just as well. In other words, if you are self-assured and positive, your dog will respond in kind.

This actively upbeat attitude will help you focus on your job—and once you begin a competition, your only job is to lead. After all, your dog is trained, you have done all you can to prepare for this day and you are ready to rock 'n roll!

So you absolutely need to be strong, you need to be composed, and you need to be focused. This attitude will go far in putting you in charge of your performance.

Taking charge means that:
YOU know what you need to do even before you enter the ring.
YOU are prepared.
YOU are directing your performance.
YOU are in control.

Taking charge means that you become **The Ring Master**.

Mastering the ring is the ultimate conclusion of all your work, all the time spent on training and getting it right. It's as though you have been making little scenes along the way and are now going to put them all together into a movie.

Try to make it an Oscar Winning Appearance!!!

7.1 PARTNERSHIP REQUIRED...

All too frequently I have seen a well-trained dog be taken into competition—and bomb. The handler is devastated and the poor dog has that deer in the headlights look: just stunned.

Why?

I've come to realize that there is no 'one size fits all' answer. Nevertheless, there are some common threads that I've noticed often enough to conclude that there are steps handlers can take to offset such a disaster—given that the dog is, indeed, properly trained.

Again, attitude and attention play an enormous role in sustaining the teamwork you have worked so long and patiently to achieve.

One obvious blunder I've often noticed in these situations is that the handler is so nervous and so terrified that she forgets to be the leader her dog needs her to be. The pair goes into the ring and there is no connection between the two: the two are no longer partners, no longer a team.

Do not throw the baby out with the bathwater! In other words, now that you are actually going to compete, you don't want to take your dog into a performance without being the leader he needs you to be.

Just because you're now competing does not mean your dog is suddenly on his own because he knows what to do. On the contrary: he needs you now more than ever.

Too often handlers take on the attitude that "My dog is trained. He knows what to do," and then abandon the dog to work it out alone.

Showing is not a sink or swim situation. This is teamwork. You need to be the leader he has come to follow and depend upon!

Go into the ring focused on being there for your dog; go into the arena proud of your accomplishments to date; go in to perform with the attitude that come hell or high water, you will be there for your dog and that no matter what happens, you'll work as a team. Keep the link and the joy of teamwork going no matter what.

> ### Be the leader your dog needs you to be!

So let's examine a few points and approaches you can adopt and utilize before and during your competition...

7.2 PREPARATION: A KEY INGREDIENT

There is no argument that the social side of competition venues is an enormous drawing card. We all like to socialize with friends, powwow, catch-up on each other's news, commiserate, gossip. It's a viable part of the dog world.

Certainly one of the reasons I personally enjoy dog shows is to meet up with friends and spend time with them. This aspect is extremely important to me.

But...it is also an intoxicating distraction that can unwittingly undermine a person's concentration and focus. To lead you need to be focused!

One approach is certainly to take charge of your destiny. Do not leave it to chance. Make all the preparations necessary for you and your partner to succeed to the best of your ability each and every time you show.

There are many things you can do to help you ultimately gain control of your performance before ever even getting to the show grounds.

> *Preparation is a key ingredient to your success!*

You need to do everything you can to make performing as pleasant and successful as is possible. Much can be accomplished before the competition, including a day to...

7.3 DESENSITIZE TO THE TRIAL ENVIRONMENT

Imagine that you are a small child playing quietly in your backyard. Suddenly a great hand reaches down out of nowhere and takes hold of your shirt collar, lifts you up and transports you across the skies, then unceremoniously deposits you smack in the middle of Time Square.

This would be a tremendous shock. It would be utterly terrifying. At the very least it would take quite a bit of regrouping to adjust and gather your composure.

Such is true with our dogs as well. We take them out of their known territory, put them in a crate and drive or fly them to a strange destination, situate them in the midst of hundreds if not thousands of other dogs—and then expect them to perform. Please...

Dogs are territorial—which is why they protect the home front. If a dog is not accustomed to traveling and working in strange places, this can prove very disorienting, even ruinous. Worse, in some cases it can so unnerve the dog that all confidence is lost, only to be replaced by a permanent negative association such as fear, panic, anxiety, even dread. Others might become defensive and develop aggressive behaviors.

It is your responsibility as your dog's leader to accustom your dog to trial environments long before you ever consider performing so that he can go into competition well adjusted and self-assured.

Consider the Canine Trinity™!

Sight, Sound, Smell: all of these senses are on high alert when your dog is on the show grounds. If your dog is not familiar and *accepting* of the dog event environment, these senses could overload and cause irreparable damage.

As soon as you deem it safe (your dog has the necessary vaccinations, etc.), begin taking him everywhere you can. And I mean everywhere. This includes pet shops, shopping centers, parks, lakes, places with loud noises such as airports or where there are children laughing, crying and screaming, on an elevator, up and down stairs, etc. And of course begin taking him to dog events. Introduce him to the world at large and allow him to soak it in and adapt.

If your dog is exhibits undue fear in any given situation, encourage him to investigate, to touch, to **not** be afraid. Do not say "It's okay." In his mind what you are doing is endorsing his fear: you're saying it's okay to be afraid. This is the exact opposite of what you are trying to do!

Rather than say 'It's okay', tell him in a teasing, confident voice to 'get it' or 'go touch' as you tap the umbrella or fire hydrant or whatever it is that is causing your young dog to worry. Once he does touch it, congratulate him! Bolster his ego, his confidence. Tell him what a brave dog he is.

Naturally some dogs are more fearful of things than others. Be patient. Do not push the dog to a breaking point.

Look for small incremental improvements and gradually, day by day, repeat the above until you have success.

Years ago I inherited an adult Doberman that was afraid of men. Toting a box of dog biscuits, I took him to the local Fire Department and asked the men on duty to please offer my Doberman a biscuit. At first my Doberman wanted nothing to do with them, but slowly, day by day, he began to trust <u>me</u>. I was patient and encouraging, but I did not baby him. It took <u>three months</u>(!), but finally this dog trusted me enough to allow men near him and to touch him— and he was comfortable with it. We never looked back.

PATIENCE...

This approach will also build your dog's trust in you. He will learn to have faith in you and follow unquestioningly.

The more your dog is introduced to different environments and experiences, the stronger and better adjusted he will become.

This will give your team a definite advantage when competing: you will have more flexibility and greater confidence.

The unknown is scary for all of us—including our dogs—which is why we are at ease with routine. It's stable; it's comfortable.

Change disrupts that comfort zone.

But the more frequently you venture out, the more comfortable doing so becomes. The more frequently a dog experiences a dog show, the more comfortable and accepting the dog becomes.

Dax is very comfortable in his crate!

It's important to realize that each and every dog show is going to have a different impact on the dog's senses. Every dog event has different smells, sounds, people, climate, weather, etc. Dogs need to be capable of tolerating change and adapting easily.

You need to condition your dog to change by acclimating him to change as often as you are able!

Condition your dog to change!

7.4 FINDING YOUR 'SHOW GAUGE'

When I arrive on any show grounds, once I am set up I will then take my dog for a small walk. Obviously I do this so that he can relieve himself if necessary, but also to give him time to assimilate the new sights, sounds, and smells—the 'Canine Trinity'™.

And yes, during this introduction, I do allow my dog to sniff. I WANT him to take it all in. I WANT him to allay his curiosity. I WANT him to familiarize himself and accept his surroundings.

Once I deem he has soaked in enough ambiance and is comfy, we play!

It is my contention that a dog that can play in an unfamiliar environment is comfortable enough to perform—given that he is sound in his training, of course.

The dog that can play in an unfamiliar place is a dog that is feeling at ease. This dog is not feeling threatened by the unknown or worried that a bogeyman will get him.

Play is my dip stick: it's my show gauge.

If my dog is willing to play, I am confident he is feeling secure enough to perform. This does not mean that our performance is going to be perfect. That's another issue☺. His playing simply indicates to me that I am not taking a frightened, worried, unhappy dog into the ring—something I would <u>never</u> do.

Obviously at a dog show my first priority is to make sure my dog is capable of performing. His willingness to play is my green light. We can go for it!

Play is my gauge, but naturally this would not be a serviceable gauge for every team. Learn to read your dog! Pay attention to your dog's reactions, body language, ear set.

It's very obvious that this dog is quite at ease in a show environment!

Find your dog's measure, be it the light in his eyes (concern or eagerness!), shoulder stature (is he slinking, tight, relaxed?), tail set (tucked in fear, on high alert, or flowing naturally?) or his ability to take food.

It is your responsibility as the team leader to make sure your dog is not only trained so that he can perform with confidence, but that he is comfortable in a trial environment. Believe me, he is telling you all you need to know: you simply have to look! Learn to interpret what he is telling you.

This ability to read your dog will all unfold as your teamwork develops through your training and your facility to truly look at your dog: you must have the proper **ATTITUDE** & pay close **ATTENTION**.

***Learn to read your dog! Study your dog's reactions and interpret what he is telling you.
Be patient, be objective. Pay attention and LOOK.***

7.5 TO ENTER OR NOT TO ENTER? THAT IS THE QUESTION.

There's a performance event coming up that you'd really like to enter. It's very tantalizing. All of your friends are going.

What to do, what to do?

First of all, be very honest with yourself. Are you and your dog really ready? Consider: you have been training for months, possibly years. Are you willing to sacrifice your goals and perhaps your future performances just because you're impatient? Because your friends will be there?

I would think not. Go, certainly. Take your dog and socialize him, acclimate him to the environment. Cheer for your friends. But be patient…

Here are some suggestions to help with that decision-making process:

- ✓ Do not send an entry in if you only think you 'might' be ready in the time left to you before the actual show date. Take charge of your future!

- ✓ Practice course or ring run-throughs with no treats, toys, or hitches. Get a feel for the upcoming real event so that you're better prepared.

- ✓ ONLY send in the entry when you are convinced your dog fully understands his job.

- ✓ ONLY send the entry in when you believe you and your dog are a team.

- ✓ Enter once your dog is working to your satisfaction in at least 5 practice matches and/or in 5 different locations and is qualifying to your level of satisfaction.

Certainly the biggest favor you can do for yourself and your dog is NOT to enter until you believe you are ready.

> # *Do Not Be a Victim: Be in Charge!*

Avoid the enticement of entering a trial before you are really ready. Be patient. By all means join your friends at the trials. Share their excitement and observations. Watch other teams compete. Learn. Socialize your dog to the show environment. You can enjoy one another's company while furthering your dog's conditioning.

And then when you believe you and your dog are ready to compete at the standard you have set for yourself (your 'Perfect Picture'), then by all means go for it!

7.6 THE 'GOLDILOCKS' SYNDROME

Now that you've sent your entry in, it's important that you don't start training too differently than what you have been doing all along.

I've come to notice two very different responses from handlers once the entry is sent in:

1.) They panic and suddenly realize that their performance has huge gaps that need fixed before they show…

OR

2.) They relinquish their leadership position to the dog, indulging and mollycoddling the dog in hopes that he will please, please, please do it right.

Sadly when the first occurs (the handler panics, gets worried, is freaking out), many of these handlers start coming down on the dog and suddenly get really tough. They drill too hard, don't praise, overwork, forget to play, are more stern, more demanding, and ultimately cause great confusion in their poor dog.

This handler has become too 'hot'.

Obviously this is not a healthy, productive approach. It is truly a poor attitude and in many cases can actually cause the dog to shut down entirely.

> **By being too 'hot,' you are changing the rules.**
>
> **By being too 'cold,' you are taking away the rules.**
>
> **Be constant.**

Conversely there's the handler who now babies the dog. This handler allows errors to occur in training with no redirection or acknowledgement of the mistake. Most will even PRAISE the dog for the error, fearing that by telling the dog he's wrong or doing anything even approaching a correction that they will cause their dog to loose his drive and 'want to'.

Actually what is now happening is that the handler, who has worked very long and hard at establishing teamwork, is now giving up the leadership position. By allowing the dog to become sloppy and basically do whatever it wants, the dog is now in control. The dog is leading the performance.

The handler that suddenly stops showing the dog how to do the job correctly is a handler that is being utterly unfair to the dog.

This handler has become too 'cold'.

If either of these attitudes is adopted, the dog will undoubtedly begin to show signs of confusion—and why not? By being too 'hot', you've changed the rules; by being too 'cold,' you've taken away the rules. The dog is left hanging. Without guidance, without a leader, your dog will not know what to do. It's no wonder the dogs become confused!

The handler's job is to **SHOW THE DOG HOW TO SUCCEED,** to sustain clarity and be a consistent trainer.

Once the entry is sent in, by all means work at fixing any 'leaks' you discover in your training, but do not allow your attitude and approach to become too hot or too cold.

If you suddenly get panicky or recognize that your dog isn't really as ready as you originally thought, pull from the trial. Don't attend.

Just because you've sent in an entry does not mean you are obligated in any way to actually go. The entry is just that: it gives you entry should you wish to attend. But it is NOT a binding contract. No one is going to come and arrest you if you do not show.

The best thing you can do for yourself once you've sent the entry in is to maintain your training status quo. Do not become too hot of a trainer or too cold of one: be normal.

Praise when merited; stop and redirect unwanted behaviors. Show your dog what it is you want him to do in an even, matter-of-fact manner. Have a positive attitude and maintain your leadership position.

This is a handler who would be 'Just right.'

7.7 BEFORE THE TRIAL DAY

Here are some pre-show ideas of things you can do to heighten your dog's competence while enjoying the process:

1. Do some proofing. Add some light challenges and distractions to your training routine that stimulate your dog's thought process without destroying his confidence. Make your dog stronger, not weaker!

2. Exercise your dog more. Build his stamina. Physical stamina will greatly increase his mental stamina, which he will need in competition.

Proofing Kyle's recall through a channel of target plates holding food. He doesn't even hesitate!

3. Sustain your normal training schedule. This is no time to increase or decrease your timetable. Keep your training 'Just right.'

4. The last week before a trial when training, stay level-headed and on an even keel. Sustain your precision, but do <u>not</u> try to introduce something new or better. The timing is all off. Keep your level of training and sustain your dog's attitude/confidence. Remember: generally there are no quick fixes, no band aides. Do the best you can without undermining a promising performance.

5. Finally, do not train the day before the trial.

   a. A day of rest is good for both you and your dog.

   b. You may unwittingly work something to death, causing your dog to worry and so not be self-assured. If this happens, it's almost guaranteed that your dog will take this self-doubt/confusion into the ring. This attitude makes for a very sad performance☹.

7.8 IT'S SHOWTIME!

The day of the trial has finally arrived.

For the sake of all the hours of training and preparation but especially for the sake of your teamwork, which you have worked very patiently and long to establish, you want to be in control of this day. It's all up to you.

You have much to do on this day. From the moment you hit the show grounds and until you have finished competing, you need to begin your strategies: you want to optimize your success; you want to sustain your mental fortitude.

You have to be the Ring Master.

7.8.1 ARRIVE EARLY

One of the first things you need to do is arrive at the event early. Do NOT get there at the eleventh hour, rip your dog out of his crate, throw him into the competition without any transition time, and then expect to do well.

Arrive in ample time to prepare you and your dog for your performance. You want to go in with focus and purpose. You do not want to enter the competition rushed, unprepared, and at the mercy of chance. Be in control!

At the very least, arrive an hour before your show time. When making your calculations of when you think you will be competing, be sure to account for possible absentees. Do not assume that everyone will show up. Make allowances for unforeseen contingencies. Be in charge!

7.8.2 SET UP FOR SUCCESS!

When you arrive, find a site that best suits your dog. That's right, your dog.

If you have a dog that gets over-stimulated by a lot of activity or is unable to relax when there is a lot of 'stuff' going on around him, move away. Set up where your dog can be comfortable. It's important that your dog have a place of refuge, of security, of down time.

Your dog is counting on you. Make the day as easy as is possible!

If your dog is not disturbed by external activity, then set up where it's most convenient for you. But first consider what is best for your partner! You are in control: your dog has no say in it.

173

It's up to you to do what is best for your dog.

Likewise, if you are the type of person who can lose confidence watching others compete, believing that you just don't have a chance against such stiff competition, don't watch. That's right. Ignore the competition until after you've finished your own performance.

If you enter the ring convinced that you can't possibly do well, you won't. You've lost already. You might as well pack up and go home.

You need to go in with a proper attitude!

- Go in knowing that your team is ready to the level that you've trained to.
- Enter the competition with pride in what you've accomplished.
- Stay mentally focused and on course.
- Be in charge and be there for your canine partner through every step of your performance.
- Be strong. Your dog is depending upon your leadership.
- Most of all, **believe in yourself and your dog.**

So if external distractions or other performances can undermine your focus, work at avoiding all interference until you've done what you've come to do, and that is compete.

Be in charge: Be the Ring Master!

7.8.3 THE 'RIGHT STUFF'

I can't tell you how many times I've run into an acquaintance at a trial and have her begin the conversation with excuses about their upcoming performance—and they haven't even been in yet.

This attitude always saddens me…

Here are two common excuses we've all heard at trials:

1. "I know we're not ready, but I just want to see where we are."

Really? I don't think so. The truth is, this person just admitted 'where they are'...**they're not ready!!!**

If you are in charge, you **know** where you are as a team. It's not guesswork, and it certainly shouldn't be an apology to other competitors.

Personally, I would never jeopardize my dog's confidence and future performances by putting him into a competition WHEN HE'S NOT READY. Doing so could set us back and ultimately cause more damage than it's worth.

Worse, going in with this attitude means that the handler doesn't believe her teammate is up to the job. It also means that it is *the dog that is being tested*—and by the team leader! How can that be? The team leader should be leading, not testing the partner.

In any performance it is the team that is being judged, not just the dog. This is well worth remembering.

2. "What will be, will be."

The handler voicing this is certainly not taking charge of the performance. This handler is casting their performance to the wind, hoping it will land somewhere in a qualifying area.

Imagine yourself driving your car up an onramp. You pull onto the freeway and immediately put the car on cruise control. Then you take your hands off the steering wheel. What will be, will be.

This is what the handler is doing when she goes into a competition with this attitude: she's no longer driving. She has removed her hands from the steering wheel. No one is in control.

Competition is teamwork. Teamwork requires that one of the members be a leader. Being a leader means that you are concentrated, you are present, you are directing the performance. Your hands are firmly fixed on that steering wheel.

Avoid carrying either of these attitudes with you when you go into a competition.

Each is a heavy load.

The weight of either one can only bring you down.

Instead arrive at the show grounds believing in yourself and your dog. **Believe!** And be there for your dog each and every step of the way.

Have the 'RIGHT STUFF'... BELIEVE!

7.8.4 GET ORGANIZED

Once you are set up and have taken care of all the busy work, it's time to think about your performance.

No matter if you are running agility, entering an obedience class, or performing in Rally, you need to know what the ring procedure will be. You should NEVER go in to perform without this knowledge.

In agility, Rally, and some obedience classes, each exhibitor is permitted to walk the course prior to the start of the class. This is a valuable asset that can be used most effectively.
Do more than simply get acquainted with the course: take advantage of it!

As you walk the course, envision your performance. FEEL your performance.

While walking the course form strategies: look for potential problem areas, areas that could be tricky to maneuver or that will require a change in your approach. Do you need to change your rhythm when reaching a particular turn, or change tactics entirely? What cues should you give your dog at this point? Make a game plan for that awkward turn or angled obstacle.

It's up to you to make these mental notes of how you need to adjust or change position or your pace at specific points in order to optimize your success.

For those competing in obedience, <u>always</u> memorize the heel pattern prior to going into the ring. Know where each exercise begins so that you can take advantage of those precious seconds in-between exercises to be focused on your dog and be able to praise him while you are moving to your next set-up.

Be in control!

No serious competitor would ever enter into a performance without either knowing the course or the heel pattern. To do so could mean disaster.

Once the course or heel pattern is made known, go off alone someplace and pantomime it without a dog. Again, picture your run in your mind as you go through the steps. Look for potentially hazardous areas that could cause you and your dog difficulties.

Imagine how you are going to handle these areas and physically *practice* what you've decided to do. Do not leave this practical side to chance. Be in charge!

Envisioning something and actually doing it are two different worlds. If I close my eyes I can imagine myself doing practically anything: I can be a rock star. I can fly to the moon. I can climb Mount Everest. In these mental dreams I'm a superstar!

In my daydreams I can win Olympics with my imaginary gymnastic skills. But in realty I can barely do a cartwheel. My only chance at ever competing at the Olympics is to first learn a skill, and then practice. This is the reality.

So do more than visualize your performance: actually walk it out. Learn it. Put it to memory. And then get a practical feel for it.

This will not only give you a better understanding of what adjustments you need to make at various points in your run, it will free you.

You won't have to think about the run while performing it. You'll already know the how and where and when. You can then give all your attentions to your main concern—your dog and being the team leader!

7.8.5 WARM-UPS

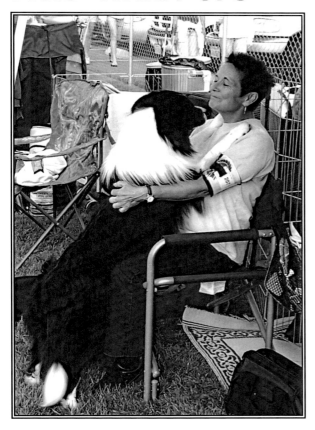

Always be sure your dog is alert and tuned into you before you go into the ring. Be prepared. Know when you will be up next and have your dog awake, eager, and anxious to get going.

If your dog will be required to jump, absolutely limber him up prior to the performance. If no practice jump is available, use a jump stick. Or have him lift up and stretch out on you. Massage his spine. He will LOVE IT!

Also move him out, let him trot a bit. You want him to be flexible and agile so that he can perform to the level you are showing.

Play is a viable and energetic way to invigorate your dog's mental alertness. Interactive play is also a terrific way of keeping your dog focused on you. If your dog is engaged in play with you, he is not going to be seeking amusement elsewhere or getting distracted or getting worried. Interactive play gives the dog a physical outlet as well as keeping him totally connected with you.

Play also energizes your dog. He will be alert. He will be alive. And he will be totally into you. You will be entering your competition with an enormous advantage: you will be entering the competition as a team!

Remember: you have entered the trial because you are ready. There is really no need to **train** on the grounds. Your dog is already trained. A warm-up, however, can be most fruitful.

A warm-up is just that: a small reminder, perhaps a bit of fine tuning. The warm-up should be short and sweet and upbeat.

Do not 'warm-up' so long and hard that you leave your best performance outside the ring. The last thing you want to do is go in with a worried, tired dog that looks like he wants to be anywhere else but with you. This is not the best strategy.

What you might want to do after limbering your dog up is to maybe refresh him on some skill, or at the very least put him in the proper frame of mind. You might want to remind him about 'left' & 'right', or perhaps a few 'fronts', or a 'stand'. Release him to a reward, interact a bit, and go into your ring with confidence and conviction. You are "Ready!"

Be as focused on your dog as you expect from your dog in return. Should someone come up while you are playing with your dog and tell you what a beautiful dog you have and so on, thank them and **MOVE AWAY.**

Do not begin a conversation with anyone or get distracted from your real concern, which is staying connected with your dog, both physically and mentally.

7.8.6 THE RIGHT MIND SET

CONFIDENCE IS A WINNING ATTITUDE

The moment you cross the threshold to begin your performance, you need to focus your mind entirely on your job, which is leading your partner. Zero in on the moment. Zero in on the task at hand as it arises. Be there.

Believe.

Do NOT worry about a skill or obstacle that 'might' be a problem. To do so is to be worrying about something in the future, not the immediate present. And you absolutely need to be in the present. You need to be there with and for your dog every second and every step of the way.

Zero in! Focus. Take each moment as it comes.

Besides, to worry and fret about something that 'might' happen is to demonstrate a lack of confidence. This attitude will undermine your ability to succeed. By its very nature, it limits you: an absence of confidence saps your mental effectiveness and weakens you.

Furthermore, if you do not have the strength of confidence, it's highly unlikely that your dog will have any either—and it's mandatory that your dog feels confident. Without that self-assurance your dog will not be able to perform to the level that you have trained.

Remember: always consider the big picture. You want your dog to enjoy performing with you so that you can have a long career together. Confidence will greatly bolster your dog's enjoyment of being your team partner and make that dream a possibility.

Confidence is critical. Confidence is an inner energy. Confidence is an inner power. **Confidence is a winning attitude.**

Take a winning **attitude** into the ring. Pay **attention** to the moment and to the needs of your dog. Be a team leader—and lead.

7.9 APPROACH TO THE RING...

Naturally it is your job as team leader to know when you are on deck for judging. Do not leave this to chance or be caught off guard. Be prepared, be in control.

If you have any questions about your position in the line-up or where things stand at the moment, by all means check. Play it safe.

Someone may have had a conflict, been moved or have even pulled from the competition. It is <u>your</u> job to know when you are going to perform, <u>not</u> the ring steward's job to tell you. The steward's job is simply to assist the judge and keep the ring moving.

When you do go to the table or board to check your status, do <u>not</u> take your dog with you. Go alone. This is insurance. Should you approach the ring with your dog, you may be unwittingly and unwillingly pulled into the ring then and there.

Like I said, the steward's job is to keep the ring moving: if the next person can't be readily located, you may find yourself drafted into being next. Should this happen, you will be flummoxed, not in control, and unprepared. You will be going into the ring at a distinct disadvantage!

Be more in control.

If you don't go with a dog, you will have ample time to return to your set-up, get your dog out of his crate, wake him up and compose your mind for your upcoming performance.

Do NOT allow yourself to be rushed, coerced, or bullied. Be polite, be agreeable, but be in control. After all, this is your performance, your entry fee, your allotted ring time.

Take charge!

When you know you are on deck and will be next into the arena, prime your dog. Be sure he has relieved himself and is alert.

Because every dog is different, it will fall on you to determine how much is too much or how little is too little in his warm-up/play stimulus.

You need to learn what buttons to push to get your dog to the sharpness of his mental ambition, his desire to work, but at the same time you don't want to leave your performance outside the ring nor go into the arena with a dog that is half asleep.

It's all a balancing act—and you are the juggler!

Let the stewards know that you are next and are near at hand. Ease their burden while at the same time taking charge:

- ✓ You have established that you are next.
- ✓ You are on deck, close enough to be noticed, but not so close that your dog can become distracted.
- ✓ You and your dog are maintaining mutual focus.
- ✓ You know the course, routine, and/or heel pattern.
- ✓ You are confident.
- ✓ You are READY.

7.10 CROSSING THE THRESHOLD...

Keeping your dog focused is probably THE most important job you're going to have as you set up. The Agility dog may be too anxious to get going and not focused, not holding the start line; the Obedience dog may be overly stimulated as well—or too worried and so lose focus; likewise in Rally.

Once your team crosses the threshold, you are usually greeted by a stranger (possibly a steward taking a leash in agility or the upper classes in obedience and rally, and/or another stranger holding a clipboard.) This minor distraction can cause some dogs to become

Enter the ring as a team. Be in control!

somewhat hesitant—or get really excited. No matter the response, focus can be lost.

Here are a few ideas of things you can do to help sustain contact with your dog while setting up:

1. Talk to your dog the entire way to your set up. Stay linked. KEEP YOUR DOG FOCUSED!!!

2. In Obedience or Rally, maneuver into your setup cleanly and without fussing. Avoid having to remind your partner to 'get straight, get in, up-sit, etc." In agility be sure you stay connected with your dog at the start line without having to nag and repeat 'Wait, you wait, wait' the entire time you move away. This can ignite your dog's drive rather than keep him controlled. (Much like the "1-2-3 Game.") Rather than nitpick, take charge!

3. If the ring steward is an overbearing in-your-face type of helper, take charge: stand between your dog and the ring steward as you remove the leash and set your dog up. YOU be in control. It's your performance!

4. Remind your dog what the game is. (We're going to jump, we're going to heel, we're going to tunnel, whatever.) In Agility and Rally tell the dog what is required before each station as the team goes through the course. When setting up for an exercise in Obedience, do likewise: tell your dog what you are about to do. Give your dog a heads up!

5. Maintain visual and/or verbal contact with your dog as much as is possible throughout your performance. You're the team leader: LEAD!

6. Go into the arena poised and ready. Concentrate. Do not be hesitant or worried.

7. Use the same body language and voice that you use when training. Consistency is important!

8. Never ask more from your dog inside a ring than you can possibly accomplish outside of the ring. Be fair and honest.

9. Finally, let your dog know you are proud of him no matter what. Be there with him and for him and help him as much as is conceivably possible.

7.11 THE UNFORESEEN DELAY

Unforeseen delays happen. The judge suddenly decides a break is in order, or it's realized that the jumps haven't been changed properly, the previous dog has soiled the ring, etc. It can be almost anything, but it's unexpected.

You're primed to start and now are told to hang loose. What can you do? ***PLAY! DOODLE!***

That's right, play or doodle with your dog. Do <u>not</u> allow yourself to become peeved or deflated or upset in anyway. This will only hurt you and your approaching performance, no one else. It's really hard to regroup and get your mind straight again if you allow this to happen.

So do not allow matters outside of your control to annoy you. Do not allow circumstances beyond your control to undermine you! You want to go into your performance ready and with a positive attitude, not disconcerted and angry. Take charge.

Do just the opposite: take advantage of this break. Engage with your dog.

I personally love it when a break occurs while I'm in the ring, as I can then make the ring a fun place for my dog by playing with him.

If I still have a leash on him, we can play tugs. If the leash has already been handed off, I can do some twists or touches or passes.

Or I can doodle. (Refer to Chapter 6: Doodling with S.O.S.) My only concern will be to keep my dog from fading. Play and/or doodling engage the dog in movement and so are a wonderful means of keeping us connected.

No matter what, my job is to keep my dog from losing focus. My job is to keep my dog alert and his drive sharp. My job is my dog!

> ## *Your job is your dog!*

7.12 PRAISE IN THE RING?

During the course of your performance, let your dog know that you're proud of him. Let your dog know that you're with him 100%.

Praise!

You'll be amazed at how well your dog will respond to this interaction and actually become more attentive to your commands and direction. Best of all, your dog will ENJOY being in the ring with you. What more can you ask?!

All dogs appreciate praise, and in my estimation you can never give too much—if it is honest. Remember: no token praise, no lip service. When you offer praise, mean it.

If verbal praise is not feasible or allowed (during exercises or runs themselves, for example), use body language:

Smile!

Making eye contact and smiling at your dog is very much a kind of praise, one your dog will understand and respond to.

Moreover, smiling at your dog and letting him know you are with him all the way will also alleviate much of your own tension and make the run that much more enjoyable for you as well. Your teamwork will improve dramatically.

So remember, if it is inopportune for you to use verbal praise, use your body language and smile!

If you are in a position where you can verbally praise your dog, take advantage of it. Do so! Praise. The amount and degree of praise you proffer is going to depend upon your dog's response levels.

With a dog that gets really amped when you praise, you may want to tone it down a bit so that you have more control of your run. Naturally praise, but use less excitement in your voice. Assure your dog that you are proud of him and with him every step of the way, but do so calmly. Keep your dog eager, but not out of control.

With a dog that is by nature more subdued, you might want to be a bit more enthusiastic with your praise. Often sincere praise will bolster the less extroverted dog into a higher plane. But be careful you don't take this dog too high: you still want control in order to qualify.

Being enthusiastic does not mean you are using praise to coax your dog into performing. That would be verbal bribery! **Remember:** you have trained your dog, you have established teamwork. Do not now go into your performance and sacrifice your leadership position by begging your dog to work.

***Do not be a cheerleader in the ring.
Cheerleaders are stuck on the sidelines:
they are not players.
Be the team leader—and lead!***

Let me repeat: your praise must be HONEST. Give praise to encourage and demonstrate that you are happy with your dog. Assure your dog that you are there for him and with him and that he is a super-dog.

Do <u>not</u> use praise to verbally bribe your dog into a better mood or into eking out a performance.

Be the leader your dog needs you to be. To know that you are still in charge, in command, is great reassurance for your dog and just what he needs to help him succeed.

7.13 ENJOY THE PROCESS!

You are finally doing it. You have put in many hours of training, conditioning, and preparation—not to mention expense—and you are now going boldly where you and your canine partner have never gone before: you are entering a ring competition.

Above all else, ENJOY IT!!!

Always make the ring time positive for your dog, no matter what. Again, think of tomorrow's show, and the next and the next. You want your dog to take pleasure in competing so that the two of you have a long and enjoyable career together.

Take a positive attitude into the ring and take that same positive attitude with you when you leave the course—even if your go was not up to your expectations.

Consider future performances: make every present run a stepping stone towards that future 'picture perfect' goal.

After all, you have worked hard and long for this moment. Relish it. Pride yourself in your accomplishments. Go in to do the best job you can possibly do. And above all else, enjoy showing off the advancements and teamwork you and your dog have achieved.

Certainly learn from each experience. That's one of your duties as team leader. You need to discover your strengths and weaknesses as a team. You need to do this without emotion. Emotions will simply get in the way and blind you or cause conflicts or warp your ability to see clearly.

Be a detached observer of your own performance as you go along. Make quick mental notes of both the pros and the cons and file these away for later consideration. LEARN from your experiences each time you compete. Always strive to become better.

But above all else, make the run enjoyable for both you and your dog. You both deserve it! Besides—it is great fun!

7.14 JACKPOT!

Too often people leave the ring and simply put their dog back in a crate after a pat or two and maybe a cookie tossed at him. It seems the dog is no longer part of the picture. He's done his part, so now he's no longer important.

WRONG!

Once you have finished your run and are all leashed up, take your dog back to your set-up and give him a jackpot. As he takes each morsel that you offer, tell him what it is for.

"Good teeter." Treat. "Good heel." Treat. "Good around." Treat. And so on...

> **The concept of the jackpot is not something that is only introduced at dog trials. Remember to introduce jackpots after those preliminary run-throughs that you do prior to a trial. Do the run-through, then lead your partner back to your set-up and jackpot him, followed by interactive play.**

Once you've given the jackpot, go play! As always, *ALL GOOD THINGS COME FROM YOU*— including that jackpot and interactive play.

Do not just toss your dog back into a crate and let that be the end of it. He's your partner! Treat him as such.

Acknowledge his performance, his ability to try, his willingness to compete with you, the joy the two of you just experienced in the ring. Savor it. Wallow in it.

If the performance does not go as well as you had hoped, so be it. Look at those parts that did go well.

Make mental notes about those things that still need work and file them away for your next training session. But right then and there, you praise, you applaud, you jackpot, and you stay in touch with your dog.

Always think ahead: always think of the big picture and your future performances. In order for your dog to maintain a healthy, upbeat attitude, you need to keep a healthy, upbeat attitude. And there is always *something* in a run to be positive about. Make mental notes of the imperfections you want to work on and shelve them until your next training session. Make the show experience something your dog wants to repeat time and time again.

The jackpot and the play reward become part of the entire trial experience for your dog. Trialing is then enjoyable and something to look forward to rather than being an onerous ordeal that causes dread, diarrhea, and disorderly conduct.

You want to leave the showground with a dog that is absolutely looking forward to the next trial.

7.15 CHAPTER REVIEW

Remember: entering a competition is the pinnacle of your training efforts. You want to enter the arena with a positive attitude, control the situation as much as is possible, and do the best job you are able to do at any given trial.

In order to do so, you need to be prepared. It falls on you as team leader to make sure the path before you is as smooth and uncomplicated as is possible.

A competition ring is not a casino: you are not there to gamble. You are there to perform and do the best you can do.

You'll need to get a feel for the entire competitive process, know when you will be showing, plan your strategies, and be in charge of your fate from the moment you set foot on the show grounds. Leave as little to chance as you can.

By being in charge, you will be a stronger competitor. Your dog will sense that. This will also give your dog strength as he will know he has a leader who has purpose and direction. You are a team.

Furthermore, when you are in control you can better enjoy the process. You KNOW what to do, when to do it, etc., and you KNOW your dog is more than capable of succeeding because you have been his team partner all along. You can enter the arena focused on your dog and actually enjoy the run!

You have put in many hours of training. You have invested a lot of time and money towards reaching your goals and attaining that "Perfect Picture" you have mentally harbored and worked towards. Entering a competition is the apex of those efforts. It's the *Grand finale!*

Control your performance: take charge. Be not only physically prepared, but mentally focused as well.

In other words, become your own RING MASTER!

A Final Wag...

It's the 'going' that matters. Take special pleasure in the hours spent working with your dog, training him and watching your relationship develop and deepen.

Learn to truly look at your dog and what he is telling you: pay attention. Train with an open mind and a positive attitude. Be the leader your dog needs you to be and I can assure you, you and your partner will attain that pinnacle of accomplishment:

TEAMWORK

Got Treats?

Chapter Recap & Reminders!

CHAPTER 1: LEADERSHIP
- ➢ No Leader, No Team: It's That Simple!
- ➢ Attention Is A Two-Way Street: It Goes Both Ways!
- ➢ Say What You Mean And Mean What You Say.
- ➢ No Excuses!

CHAPTER 2: CANINE TRINITY™
- ➢ Body Language Counts.
- ➢ When Training Or Trialing, Be Sure Your Attitude Is **POSITIVE**.

CHAPTER 3: THE PERFECT PICTURE
- ➢ Always Have Quality Training Sessions.
- ➢ Be Clear, Be Consistent.
- ➢ Say What You Mean And Mean What You Say.
- ➢ Train To Trial!

CHAPTER 4: PRAISE
- ➢ Praise Is An Expression Of Approval.
- ➢ Praise Must Be Your Primary Reward!
- ➢ Teach Through Success...
- ➢ Lure To Teach: Reward A Learned Behavior.
- ➢ Apply the 4-Stage Release Program.

CHAPTER 5: PLAY & INTERACTION
- ➢ Never Allow Your Dog To Ignore You; Likewise, Never Ignore Your Dog.
- ➢ Training And Play = One!
- ➢ Interactive Play Is A Great Motivator.

CHAPTER 6: TRAIN, TRAIN, TRAIN...
- ➢ What You Have In Training Is What You Take Into The Ring.
- ➢ Be Honest And Be Fair.
- ➢ Have Quality In Your Training. Quality Is Substance.
- ➢ Keep Your *Training Alive!*™

CHAPTER 7: BECOME THE RING MASTER!
- ➢ Partnership Required!
- ➢ Discover Your "Show Gauge."
- ➢ Your Job Is Your Dog.
- ➢ Do Not Be A Victim: Be In Charge!
- ➢ Most Of All, **BELIEVE!!!**...And Enjoy The Process.

NOTES